S0-ECP-793

The Secretary's Quick Reference Handbook

Sheryl L. Lindsell

ARCO PUBLISHING, INC.
NEW YORK

Published by Arco Publishing, Inc.
215 Park Avenue South, New York, N.Y. 10003

Library of Congress Cataloging in Publication Data

Lindsell, Sheryl L.
  The secretary's quick reference handbook.

  Includes index.
  1. Secretaries—Handbooks, manuals, etc. 2. Office
practice—Handbooks, manuals, etc. I. Title.
HF5547.5.L56   1983   651.3'741'0202   82-8888
ISBN 0-668-05595-2

Printed in the United States of America

CONTENTS

Part II: Secretarial Techniques and Procedures

Part III: Professional Potpourri

PREFACE

Working in a modern office today offers excitement, stimulation, and diverse challenges. You must be prepared to meet these challenges by staying abreast of the most current methods and practices. Just as technology and business are meeting the demands of a changing society, so must you. The secretary of today is a vital, vibrant, and essential part of a team—a team that can be a positive force contributing to the effectiveness of any organization.

The career opportunities available to today's secretary are wide and varied. Regardless of your career goals, meet each task with enthusiasm, putting forth your best effort. Set your goals, learn all you can, and each day will bring you one step closer to attaining personal and professional fulfillment.

The key that will unlock doors and lead you up your career path is your ability to communicate on paper. This manual is a simplified, easy-to-use guide to correct and effective writing. It is a compilation of the latest rules, formats, and methods being used in today's office.

Sheryl L. Lindsell

Part I.
Mechanics of
English

CHAPTER 1

PUNCTUATION

Commas, Semicolons, Colons, Dashes, Parentheses, Brackets, Underscores, Quotation Marks, Ellipses, Periods, Question Marks, Exclamation Points, Apostrophes, Asterisks, Diagonals or Slashes

Woman without her man is a savage.
Woman: without her, man is a savage.

If you will note the difference in meaning between the two sentences above, you will realize the vital role punctuation plays in communicating clear and accurate messages. The following guidelines will clarify many of the punctuation problems with which you may be having difficulty.

Commas

The comma (,) is the most misused mark of punctuation. Its main purpose is to help the reader properly interpret the meaning of a sentence.

ADDRESSES AND DATES

Use commas between items in an address or date.

> We are moving our headquarters to 24 Besen Parkway, New York, New York, next month. (If the ZIP code were used in this example, a comma would not be placed after the state but would follow the ZIP.)
>
> On Sunday, August 15, 1982, Marc will be seventeen.

When using the month and year only, either surround the year with commas or omit them completely.

> In August, 1982, Marc will be seventeen.
> In August 1982 Marc will be seventeen.

APPOSITIVES

Use commas to set off expressions that explain the preceding word, name, or phrase.

> Lafayette Avenue, our town's main street, is closed for repair.
> Mr. Weston, our representative, is waiting to see you.
> Mr. Weston, of Harkness Brothers, is waiting to see you.
> My only sister, Susan, has been accepted at West Point.

CONJUNCTIONS

Use a comma before a conjunction (*and, but, for, or, nor, yet*) provided the conjunction joins two independent clauses that could otherwise be complete sentences.

George will not be here at ten but will arrive at
  eleven. (independent and dependent)
George will not be here at ten, but he will arrive at
  eleven. (independent and independent)

DIRECT ADDRESS

Use commas to set off words that directly address the person
to whom you are speaking either by name, title, or relationship.

Mr. Green, please send me a copy of that letter.
Please send me a copy of that letter, Mr. Green.
Let me tell you, fellow members, what the committee
  has done.

INTRODUCTORY CLAUSES

Use a comma after an introductory clause. Note that an
introductory clause will always be followed by what could be
a complete sentence. (Some key words are *if, since, because,
when, while, as, unless, provided, after,* and *before.*)

When we finish the chapter, we will have a test.
Because you came late, you will have to stay late.
Unless you call, I will assume you are coming.
If I hear from him, I will notify you.

Use a comma to set off an independent introductory expression that serves as an interjection.

No, I do not think he is correct.
In fact, I do not think anyone knows the answer.
You know, he may have been too shy to ask.

NONRESTRICTIVE AND RESTRICTIVE ELEMENTS

Use commas to set off expressions that if omitted would not change or destroy the meaning of the sentence.

> The woman who just entered is my sister. (Restrictive. *Who just entered* identifies which woman.)
>
> My sister, who is wearing a red coat, is an accountant. (Nonrestrictive. *Who is wearing a red coat* describes but does not change the meaning of the subject *sister.*)
>
> This magazine, *Newsweek,* is very informative. (Nonrestrictive. *Newsweek* describes the subject, *magazine,* by giving its name but does not change the meaning of the sentence.)
>
> The magazine *Newsweek* is very informative. (Restrictive. Here the name of the magazine is vital to the meaning of the sentence. The speaker or writer limits or *restricts,* the quality of being *very informative* to this one magazine in a sentence that indicates a consideration of many or all magazines.)

PARENTHETICAL EXPRESSIONS

Use commas to set off a word, phrase, or clause that interrupts the natural flow of the sentence.

accordingly	for example
as a consequence	however
as a result	I believe
as a rule	if any
as well as...	if necessary
as you know	in addition
by the way	in brief

in fact
it has been said
it seems
I understand
moreover
nevertheless

of course
on the contrary
on the other hand
therefore
to be sure
together with...

We have, I believe, two days left.
Mr. Smith, as well as his assistant, will be leaving
   early.
We will, nevertheless, proceed as scheduled.

If any of the expressions above are used in a manner that will
not interrupt the natural flow of the sentence, do not use
commas.

However experienced he may be, he will not qualify
   for the position. (*However* is part of the introductory phrase.)

QUOTATIONS

Use commas to identify a person who is being directly
quoted.

"I will not arrive until much later," he said.
He said, "I will not arrive until much later."

The comma and period at the end of quoted material always
go *inside* the quotation mark.

SERIES

Use commas to separate a series of three or more items
unless a conjunction is placed between each.

He enjoys reading and swimming. (two items)
He enjoys reading, swimming, and bowling. (three items)
He enjoys reading and swimming and bowling. (conjunctions)

In a sentence like the second example above, a comma should be placed before the final conjunction to avoid misreading. Do not use a comma before the final *and* or ampersand symbol (&) within the name of a company.

He is a member of Gold, Smith & Weston.

TITLES, DEGREES, AND ABBREVIATIONS

Use commas to set off abbreviations, titles, and degrees that follow a name. Always use commas before *Inc.* and *Ltd.*

Thomas James, Jr., is our newly elected chairman.
Max Lorenz, C.P.A., will be our guest speaker.
ABC Realty Co., Inc., is moving to the South.
Walter McNicholas, Esq., is a promising attorney.

If you use *Esq.* after the name of an attorney or *M.D.* after the name of a doctor, drop the prefixes *Mr.*, *Dr.*, etc.
Roman numerals following a person's name are not set off with commas.

Thomas James II is our newly elected chairman.

VERBALS

Use a comma following an introductory verbal phrase (a phrase beginning with an infinitive or with a verb ending *ed* or *ing*) when it is used to modify the remainder of the sentence.

To prove his point, he checked the reference book.
Provoked, he slammed the door behind him.
Lacking confidence, the boy did not enter the contest.

MISCELLANEOUS

1. Use commas to set off adjectives that follow the noun they are modifying.

   The cashier, frustrated and exhausted, located the error.

2. Use commas to set off contrasting expressions such as *not, never, seldom.*

   I saw him in March, not April.
   He always teaches sociology, never psychology.

3. Use a comma to divide a sentence that starts as a statement and ends as a question.

   You will call him, won't you? (This type of sentence will always end with a question mark.)

4. Use commas to separate items in reference works.

   You will find that information in Volume III, Chapter 2, page 12, line 2.

5. Use commas to separate words that are repeated for emphasis.

   He told me that story many, many times.

6. Use commas to clarify numerals that have four or more digits.

$1,000   4,356 votes   12,000 words

Exceptions include telephone numbers, years, serial numbers, ZIP codes, invoice numbers, policy numbers, and the like.

352-8198   Policy No. 110285641   10952 (ZIP)

7. Use commas in sentences that would be confusing if they were omitted.

Only one week before, I had lunch with him. (Without the comma, you would have a sentence fragment.)

8. Use commas to indicate that readily understood words have been omitted.

Theodore will be given $500; Susan, $300; and Bob, $200. (After *Susan* and after *Bob* the words *will be given* have been omitted.)

9. Use a comma after the complimentary closing of a letter, except when you are using open punctuation. (See the "Standard Letter Parts" section of chapter 10 for more information about open punctuation.)

Sincerely yours,   Respectfully yours,
Very truly yours,   Cordially yours,

Note that only the first word of the complimentary closing is capitalized.

10. Use a comma to separate two sets of figures that are not related.

Since 1958, 500 machines have been sold.

11. Use a comma after inverted names such as on a list or in a file.

Coleman, Russell (*Russell* is the first name.)

12. Use a comma to separate a phrase from the rest of the sentence when the phrase is inverted or taken out of its natural order.

For me, it will mean more work and less pay.

13. Use a comma to separate two adjectives in a series, provided the word *and* could be used between the two.

She is an intelligent, thoughtful person. (The word *and* could be placed between: *intelligent and thoughtful.*)
These three old manual typewriters are in need of repair. (The word *and* could not logically be placed between *three old manual.*)

Semicolons

The semicolon (;) has often been referred to as a weak period or a strong comma. It is a useful mark of punctuation, but it should be used sparingly.

1. Use a semicolon to separate independent clauses in a compound sentence when no conjunction is used to join the clauses.

You need not send any money now; we will bill you later. (Two independent clauses: *You need not send any money now. We will bill you later.*)

You need not send any money, for we will bill you later. (When a conjunction is used, a comma will separate the clauses.)

2. Use a semicolon to separate independent clauses joined by a conjunction (such as *and, but, or, nor*) if two or more commas are used in either clause and if the semicolon will prevent misreading.

I thought I had met everyone in your family; but James, the youngest, told me that you have a sister who lives in Canada.

I like red, blue, and green; but she likes brown, black, and rust.

3. Use a semicolon between coordinate clauses of a compound sentence when they are joined by transitional (parenthetical) words and phrases. (Check the list of parenthetical expressions given in the "Commas" section of this chapter.)

The jury has been deliberating for two days; however, they have not reached a decision.

President Smith has approved a new tax cut; therefore, we should start to see more money in our paychecks.

4. Use a semicolon to separate items in a series when the items themselves contain commas.

He was available on Monday, January 5; Tuesday, January 6; and Wednesday, January 7.

I will be giving special awards to Alma Kuhn, secretary; Warren Bergstein, accountant; and Fran Haber, teacher.

5. Use a semicolon before expressions such as *for example, that is, for instance, that is to say,* or *namely.*

The paint is available in three colors; namely, red, blue, and beige.

Many of our policies will change this year; for example, our salespeople will be paid on a commission basis.

Colons

The colon (:) indicates the strongest possible break in a sentence and often draws the reader's attention to that which follows.

1. Use a colon after a formal introduction that includes (or implies) the phrase *the following.*

You should know how to use the following office machines: a typewriter, a duplicator, and a calculator.

We expect to open branch offices in each of these states: California, Nevada, and Oregon. (*The following* is implied.)

You should not use a colon after the main verb in a sentence.

Her most difficult subjects are English, science, and mathematics. (*Are* is the main verb.)

2. Use a colon to introduce a long direct quotation.

   Congressman Gilroy said: "I know the importance of winning, but it is not worth your while to get yourself involved in that scheme."

3. Use a colon after a statement that introduces an explanation or an example.

   My final recommendation is this: Do not delay.

4. Use a colon after the salutation of a business letter unless you are using open punctuation (see chapter 10, "Standard Letter Parts").

   Gentlemen: Dear Mr. Jones:
   Dear Sir: My dear Miss Smith:

5. Use a colon to separate hours and minutes when expressed in figures. Omit the :00 when expressing time as an even clock hour.
   4:30 p.m.   2:45 a.m.
   3 p.m.   5 a.m.

   NOTE: Refer to the "Numbers" chapter for further rules regarding clock hours.

Dashes

   The dash (—) is a very emphatic mark of punctuation used for emphasis or visual effect. Use it sparingly, because the overuse of it diminishes its effect. When typing the dash, use

two hyphens, * and do not leave a space before, after, or in
between.

1. Use dashes to set off a parenthetical expression or an
appositive that you want to emphasize.

Have you attended a convention in New Jersey's most
famous resort—Atlantic City? (instead of comma)
The book—in case you are interested—is very informative.

2. Use a dash before a word (such as *these, any, all, each*)
that sums up a preceding series.

Pies, cheesecakes, and tarts—these are our special-
ties.
Lynne Sullivan, Janice Teisch, and Ann Kraft—these
are my friends from school.

3. Use a dash to indicate a summarizing thought or an
afterthought added to the end of a sentence.

That course was a big help to me—I liked it.
I am sure that was not an easy decision—not even
for you. (more emphasis than a comma)

4. Use a dash before the name of an author or work that
follows a direct quotation and gives its source.

"Ask not what your country can do for you. Ask what
you can do for your country."—John F. Kennedy

---

*A separate treatment of hyphens has not been included in this
chapter. For information about the uses of this punctuation mark,
see chapter 2, "Compound Adjectives"; chapter 4, "Hyphenated
Numbers"; and chapter 5, under the "Do's" of word division.

"English is undoubtedly the most important of the world's languages at the present time."—*Webster's New Collegiate Dictionary*

5. Use dashes to emphasize an independent clause that has abruptly interrupted the main thought of a sentence.

I was certain that our manager—he more than anyone else I know—would have recommended Jim for that promotion.

Parentheses

Parentheses ( ) are used in somewhat the same fashion as dashes, only they tend to de-emphasize the conveyed message. The degree of emphasis to be conveyed is the choice of the writer.

1. Use parentheses to set off parenthetical expressions or appositives that you want to de-emphasize.

She returned to New York (her favorite city) for her vacation.

2. Use parentheses to set off references to charts, pages, diagrams, illustrations, chapters of books, etc.

The section on philosophy (pages 200–260) should be very helpful to you.

3. Parentheses may be used to enclose numerals or letters that precede items in a series that are in sentence form.

The countries to be visited are (1) England, (2) France, (3) Italy, and (4) Spain.

For lists in columns, any of the following forms may be used:

1)	1.	(1)
2)	2.	(2)
3)	3.	(3)

4. Use parentheses in formal writing, such as legal documents, when the writer wants to use both the spelled-out number and the written number.

The Purchaser agrees to pay to the Seller the sum of
ONE THOUSAND and 00/100 DOLLARS
($1,000.00).

5. If the item in parentheses falls inside the sentence, the sentence punctuation should be placed outside the parentheses.

Stationery often measures 8½ by 11 inches (216 by 279 millimeters).
When you call (hopefully today), I should have the answer.

6. If the item in parentheses is a complete sentence, the mark of punctuation will go inside the parentheses.

Dr. Harold Siegelbaum is a gynecologist. (Dr. Louis Lefkowitz is a gynecologist and obstetrician.)

Brackets

Brackets ([ ]) are not always a standard key on the typewriter and may have to be inserted by hand.

1. In quoted material, use brackets to enclose anything added by someone other than the writer or speaker.

> He said, "The length of the trial [from June 15 to September 16] caused great inconvenience to the jurors."

2. Use brackets to enclose parenthetical information within a larger parenthesis.

> Your order (which included a ream of paper and a dozen pencils [markers are unavailable]) was delivered on Monday.

Keep in mind that brackets are rarely used in business writing. They are generally found in printed material.

Underscores

1. Use an underscore (_____) to set off the titles of books, magazines, newspapers, pamphlets, brochures, long poems, movies, plays, and other literary works.

> I read <u>The New York Times</u> every day.

An alternative is to completely capitalize the title.

> I read THE NEW YORK TIMES every day.

2. Use underscores with foreign expressions that may be unfamiliar to the reader.

> The attorney introduced <u>prima facie</u> evidence.

Quotation Marks

Quotation marks (" ") are extremely important marks of punctuation and must be used properly.

1. Use quotation marks to enclose material that is directly quoted; that is, the exact words of what was originally said or written.

   "I saw your advertisement in the newspaper," he said.

   Do not put quotation marks around an indirect quotation; that is, a rewording of the original statement.

   He said that he had seen your advertisement in the newspaper.

2. Use quotation marks to enclose titles of articles, short poems, lectures or topics, paintings, short stories, or chapter names of books. Check the chapter on "Capitalization" for further rules.

   In *Webster's Legal Secretaries Handbook* there is a very informative chapter entitled "Preparing and Typewriting Client Documents."

3. Unless otherwise punctuated, use quotation marks to set off words or phrases introduced by any of the following expressions: *the word, the term, known as, marked, termed, called, entitled.*

   The check was marked "cancelled."

4. Use quotation marks around familiar words used in an unusual or unconventional manner.

   My brother thinks he is "hot stuff."

5. Use single quotation marks to set off a quotation that appears within a quotation.

   The student asked, "How do I spell the word 'accommodate'?"

6. When quoting lengthy material, you should place the quotation mark at the beginning of each paragraph and at the end of the final paragraph only.

   " _____
   _____
   _____ .

   " _____
   _____
   _____ ."

QUOTATION MARKS AND OTHER PUNCTUATION

1. Always place the period and comma *inside* the quotes.

   He commented, "They already left."
   "They already left," he commented.

2. Always place the semicolon and colon *outside* the quotes.

   He said, "I will see you about noon"; however, it is already one.

3. A question mark and exclamation point will go inside the quoted material when it applies to the quoted material *only*. It will go outside when it applies to the entire sentence.

She asked, "Did you enjoy your trip?" (The quoted
material alone is the question, not the entire sentence.)

Why did you call me "impossible"? (The entire sentence is a question.)

Ellipses

Use an ellipsis (...) to indicate what words are being
omitted from the original quoted material. Space once before,
between, and after each period. If indicating the omission of
the end of a sentence, a complete sentence, or more, use four
periods (....).

"Let everyone mind his own business, and endeavor
to be what he was made. ... If a man does not
keep pace with his companions, perhaps it is because he hears a different drummer. Let him step
to the music which he hears, however measured
or far away."—Thoreau

Periods

The period (.) is probably the most common punctuation
mark.

1. Use the period at the conclusion of a statement, a request
   (even when phrased politely as a question), or command.

   I very much appreciate your consideration.
   May I hear from you at your earliest convenience. (a
   polite request)

2. Use the period in writing some abbreviations. (Many abbreviations are now being used without the period.)

Dr.	Mrs.	Ph.D.
Inc.	Co.	a.m.
FBI	YMCA	NAACP
NATO	TVA	CIA

When a sentence ends with an abbreviation, one period is used which represents both the abbreviation and the end of the sentence.

I purchased my sofa from A & D Interiors, Inc.

3. The period is used as a decimal point.

Our profits have increased by 13.5 percent.

4. Use the period to separate dollars from cents.

I purchased the blouse for $28.50.

Question Marks

1. Use a question mark to conclude a direct question.

When may we expect you?

2. Use a question mark after each question in a series of short questions that relate to the same subject and verb.

Can you join us on March 16? March 17? March 18?

3. Use a question mark when a sentence begins as a statement and ends as a question.

> You made the delivery, didn't you?

4. Use a question mark in parentheses to indicate uncertainty about a stated fact.

> You ordered ten (?) copies of the book.

5. If a question ends with an abbreviation, place the question mark after the period.

> Did you purchase that at ABC Stores, Inc.?

Exclamation Points

The exclamation point (!) is used after a word or group of words that express strong feelings (such as anger, relief, fear, excitement, surprise).

> That is an absolutely incredible story!
> "Look out!" the man shouted.

Apostrophes

The apostrophe (') is used primarily to indicate an omission or to show possession.

1. Use an apostrophe to indicate that there has been an omission in a number or a word.

> '75 (1975)
> didn't (did not)
> I've (I have)

In formal writing, however, it is proper to avoid contractions, when possible.

Formal: I will call as soon as I have returned.
Informal: I'll call as soon as I've returned.

2. Form the possessive of a singular noun by adding an apostrophe and an *s*.

the cat's meow	the baby's bottle
Sue's coat	Mr. Jones's car
your boss's desk	the lady's umbrella

3. Form the possessive of a plural noun that ends in *s* by adding an apostrophe only.

two cats' food	the babies' bottles
the girls' coats	the Joneses' car
your bosses' desks	the ladies' umbrellas

4. Form the possessive of an irregular plural noun (one that does not end in *s*) by adding an apostrophe and an *s*.

your teeth's condition	children's toys
women's hats	oxen's hoofs
salespeople's commissions	foremen's influence

5. Use the apostrophe in common expressions referring to time, distance, value, or measurement.

yesterday's news	a moment's notice
a month's vacation	three months' vacation
five miles' distance	a year's salary

6. Use the apostrophe after the period in order to make an abbreviation possessive.

> The M.B.A.'s thesis
> ABC Realty Co.'s contracts
> the M.D.'s opinion

7. Use the apostrophe to indicate possession at the end of a compound word.

> sister-in-law's car
> sisters-in-law's cars
> the secretary-treasurer's report
> everybody's responsibility

8. Use the apostrophe to indicate the plural form of numbers, letters, and symbols.

> He has three i's in his name.
> He gave me three 20's as
> change.

9. Use the apostrophe after the last of two or more nouns in order to indicate joint ownership.

> Judy and Joan's locker
> Joe and Al's car

10. Use the apostrophe after each noun in order to indicate individual ownership.

> Judy's and Joan's lockers
> Joe's and Al's cars

11. The apostrophe is generally omitted in names of organizations, magazines, etc.

> State Teachers College
> Bankers Trust Company

Asterisks

The asterisk (*) is used infrequently.

1. Use the asterisk to refer the reader to a footnote at the bottom of the page.

   "It's been noted of Vermont winters that when one isn't currently in progress, one either will be shortly or was recently."*

2. Use the asterisk to indicate the omission of words that are unfit for printing or the omission of an entire paragraph.

   How dare you call him a •••!
   It is of no consequence to Sir Thomas whether or not her visit proves enjoyable so long as she learns to respect the wealth that she has lived in at Mansfield.

   *   *   *

   Jane's stay at Portsmouth does, in fact, make her long for her childhood home, though not for the reasons Sir Thomas had intended.

Diagonals or Slashes

1. Use the diagonal or slash (/) in certain abbreviations and expressions of time.

---

*Brian Vachon, "Winter in Vermont," *Vista*, Winter 1981–82, p. 4.

c/o (care of)   3/4 (fraction)
B/L (bill of lading)   1979/80

2. Use the diagonal for *and/or* expressions.

   Sales/advertising will be located in this office.

CHAPTER 2

GRAMMAR

Adjectives, Adverbs, Conjunctions, Nouns, Prepositions, Pronouns, Verbs, Super Stumpers, Subject and Verb Agreement

Grammar, as defined in *Webster's New Collegiate Dictionary*, is "the study of the classes of words, their inflections, and their functions and relations in the sentence..." This chapter presents in alphabetical order the major parts of speech with explanations and examples of correct usage.

Adjectives

An adjective is a word, a phrase, or a clause that either modifies, describes, or limits the noun or pronoun it is describing. When used properly, the adjective can transform an ordinary sentence into a very colorful one.

> The darkly charred steak sizzled on the grill—its top
> beaded with hot, red juices.
> *as opposed to*
> The steak cooked on the grill.

An adjective will answer the questions: What kind? Which? What color? How many? What size?

red dress   *rainy* day
this book   *five* dozen
good friend   *less* expensive
linen curtains   *difficult* task
several ideas

Adjectives take different forms according to the noun or nouns they modify. The positive degree is the form of the adjective used when no comparison is being made. The comparative degree is the form of the adjective that compares two things or people. The superlative degree compares three or more things or people.

Positive	Comparative	Superlative
big	bigger	biggest
cold	colder	coldest
pretty	prettier	prettiest
young	younger	youngest
heavy	heavier	heaviest
fine	finer	finest

When the positive adjective is one syllable, an *er* forms the comparative degree and an *est* forms the superlative degree. This rule also holds true for some two syllable words. For many words ending in y, you must change the y to i and add *er* or *est*. When the positive adjective is two syllables or more, you most often use *more* or *less* with the comparative degree and *most* or *least* with the superlative degree. *More* and *most* indicate increasing amounts and *less* and *least* indicate decreasing amounts.

Positive	Comparative	Superlative
active	more active	most active
	less active	least active

successful	more successful	most successful
	less successful	least successful
careful	more careful	most careful
	less careful	least careful
capable	more capable	most capable
	less capable	least capable
fortunate	more fortunate	most fortunate
	less fortunate	least fortunate

That is a *big* building.
That building is the *bigger* of the two.
That building is the *biggest* of all.
He is a *successful* actor.
He is a *more successful* actor than his brother.
He is the *most successful* actor in our group.

A few adjectives have irregular comparative and superlative degrees.

Positive	**Comparative**	**Superlative**
good or well	better	best
far (distance)	farther	farthest
far (degree)	further	furthest
much or many	more	most
little (amount)	less	least
little (size)	littler	littlest
bad or ill	worse	worst

Some adjectives, because of their meaning, are absolute and cannot be compared.

dead	genuine
exact	always
square	perfect
impossible	round
unique	wrong

> never   correct
> empty   accurate
> stationary

NOTE: If something is *exact*, for example, that is an absolute degree. A thing cannot be more or less exact.

COMPOUND ADJECTIVES

In many cases it is necessary to join two adjectives together (using a hyphen) so that they form a single description.

> I have twenty-one dollar bills. ($21)
> I have twenty one-dollar bills. ($20)
> a light-blue coat
> a part-time job
> bumper-to-bumper traffic

To require a hyphen, the adjective must come before the noun it is modifying.

> That is a well-written report.
> That report is well written.

Use more than one hyphen when an idea has one noun ending but two or more adjectives to describe it.

> a two- or three-year lease
> a part- or full-time job
> a 50-, 60-, or 70-person capacity

Note the spacing and the use of commas above.

Exceptions to this rule are as follows:

1. Do not use a hyphen between adjectives if the first adjective ends in *est* or *ly*. (a newly completed house, the freshest cut flowers)

2. Do not use a hyphen between a number and the word *percent*. (a ten percent discount)
3. Do not use a hyphen with expressions that you automatically think of as one, such as *social security tax, real estate office, word processing system, life insurance policy. Coordinate Adjectives:* When two or more adjectives are not joined by *and, or,* or *nor* and they are modifying the same noun, a comma will take the place of the conjunctions.

an efficient, reliable secretary
an efficient and reliable secretary
a sincere, intelligent face
a sincere and intelligent face
a long, winding road
a long and winding road

If the word *and* does not sound right between the adjectives, omit the comma.

I purchased a new green car. (Although *new* and *green* are adjectives, you would not say *a new and green car.*)
Her bright red dress complemented her shiny black hair.

ARTICLES

The adjectives *a* and *an* are also called indefinite articles. They are indefinite because they do not refer to a specific object; for example, *the book* is specific whereas *a book* is not.

The use of *a* or *an* is determined by the *sound* of the word that immediately follows. If the word begins with a consonant sound, use the article *a*. If the word begins with a vowel sound, use the article *an*.

a device	a unique design
a mile	an onion
a two-week trip	an heir (vowel sound)
a home	an X-ray (vowel sound)
a high level	an error
a call	an illness

Adverbs

An adverb is a word that modifies a verb, an adjective, or another adverb. It answers the questions: How? When? Why? How much? Where? To what degree?

Adverbs take different forms for the positive, comparative, and superlative degrees. The positive degree is the form of the adverb used when no comparison is being made. The comparative degree is the form of the adverb used for comparing two things. The superlative degree compares three or more things.

Positive	Comparative	Superlative
fast	faster	fastest
effectively	more effectively	most effectively
	less effectively	least effectively

Many adjectives function as adverbs as well. Many remain the same in both forms; others require the addition of *ly*.

His handwriting is *legible*. (adjective)
He writes *legibly*. (adverb)
The senator's speech was *brief*. (adjective)
The senator spoke *briefly*. (adverb)

Adverbs are used to describe the senses (see, taste, feel, smell, and hear). Adjectives are used to describe these verbs when the modifier refers to the condition of the subject.

The red rose smells *sweet*. (adjective referring to condition)

The *sweetly* scented perfume had a very strong odor. (adverb describing the adjective *scented*)

DOUBLE NEGATIVES

Never use two negative words to express a single negative idea.

Right: We *do not* require *any* more information.
Wrong: We *do not* require *no* more information.
Right: I can *hardly* believe my eyes.
Wrong: I *can't hardly* believe my eyes.

Remember that *hardly* and *scarcely* express a negative idea— no other negative word is necessary in sentences in which either one appears.

Two of the most commonly confused adjectives and adverbs are *real* and *really* and *good* and *well*.

real (adjective meaning *genuine*)
really (adverb meaning *actually*)

Are you wearing *real* cowboy boots?
I had a *really* good time at the party.

good (adjective meaning *praiseworthy*)
well (adverb referring to health)

You did a *good* job repairing the chair.
I do not feel *well* today.

Conjunctions

A conjunction is a word that connects two words, phrases, or clauses. Three types are coordinate, correlative, and subordinate.

COORDINATE CONJUNCTIONS

These are used to join two or more words, phrases, or clauses that are equal in construction and grammatical rank.

and	but
or	nor
for	yet
so	whereas (legal term)

I read the book, *and* I enjoyed it very much.
I read the book *and* enjoyed it very much.

NOTE: For comma rules accompanying conjunctions, refer to the "Punctuation" chapter.

CORRELATIVE CONJUNCTIONS

These are used in pairs and join the elements of a sentence.

both/and	either/or
so/as	neither/nor
not only/but also	as/as
whether/or	whether/or not

I have read *neither* his report *nor* his letters.
Both Paula *and* her sister are out at a movie.

SUBORDINATE CONJUNCTIONS

These connect a subordinate (dependent) clause to the main clause. The clauses they introduce always function as adverbs, adjectives, or nouns within a complete sentence. The following are commonly used subordinate conjunctions:

after	provided that
although	since
as	so . . . as
as . . . as	so that
as if	than
as long as	that
as soon as	though
as though	till
because	unless
before	until
even if	when
even though	whenever
except	where
if	wherever
in order that	whether
provided	while

Please tell me *when* the group arrives. (*When* serves as a subordinate conjunction and does not have a comma placed before it.)

When the group arrives, please tell me. (An adverb clause introduced with a subordinate conjunction does require a comma.)

Nouns

A noun is a person, a place, or a thing and can be either proper or common. A proper noun should be capitalized and a common noun should not.

Proper Nouns	Common Nouns
New York City	city
Royale Theater	theater
Spring Valley High School	high school
Main Street	street

A **collective noun** identifies a group, company, council, audience, faculty, union, team, jury, committee, etc. When the group is acting as a unit, use a singular verb; when the group is acting as independent members, use a plural verb.

The *family is* going to Cancún for vacation.
The *family are* going on separate vacations this year.
The *jury is* deliberating.
The *jury are* going home.

NOTE: Refer to the "Spelling" chapter for the formation of plural nouns.

Prepositions

A preposition is a connecting word that shows the relationship between words in a sentence.

above	below	in
about	beneath	inside
across	beside	into
after	between	like
against	beyond	near
along	by	of
among	down	off
around	during	on
at	except	since
before	for	to
behind	from	toward

through	up	within
under	upon	
until	with	

Listed below are some commonly confused prepositions:

accompany by (a person)
accompany with (an object)

> Mrs. Jones was *accompanied by* her son.
> The carriage was *accompanied with* assembling instructions.

account for (something or someone)
account to (someone)

> I cannot *account for* his behavior.
> The cashier had to *account to* the manager for the shortage.

agree to (somcone else's plan)
agree with (have same opinion)

> I will *agree to* the terms of our contract.
> I *agree with* you about the terms of our contract.

angry at or about (something)
angry with (someone)

> He was *angry about* the outcome of the discussion.
> I hope you will not be *angry with* me.

apply for (a position)
apply to (someone or something)

> I am going to *apply for* the job in the newspaper.
> I am going to *apply to* that company for a job.

argue about (something)
argue with (someone)

> I do not want to *argue about* the problem.
> I do not want to *argue with* you about the problem.

compare to (show similarity)
compare with (examine for similarities and differences)

> You can *compare* that restaurant *to* the best.
> She *compared* my acting *with* Marilyn Monroe's.

compensate for

> The attorney was *compensated for* his time.

comply with

> Will you *comply with* the orders?

consists in (exists in)
consists of (comprised of)

> Happiness *consists in* knowing you are loved.
> The books *consists of* 15 chapters.

convenient for (suitable)
convenient to (close)

> Will Monday morning be *convenient for* you?
> The new shopping center should be *convenient to* all
>   forms of transportation.

correspond to (agree with)
correspond with (write letters)

> The merchandise does not *correspond to* your ad.
> I *correspond with* my pen pal regularly.

depend on (rely)

> You can *depend on* me to get the job done.

differ about (something)
differ from (to be unlike)
differ with (someone)

> We *differ about* ways to perform the task.
> I *differ from* you in many ways.
> I *differ with* you over the projected outcome.

different from (never *than*)

> This new typewriter is *different from* the one I had.

encroach on (infringe on)

> The pool *encroaches on* your neighbor's property.

indicative of

> This attempt is *indicative of* my capabilities.

liable for (responsible)
liable to (susceptible)

> You will be *liable for* any damage to my car.
> You are *liable to* have a heart attack if you do not
>   slow down.

parallel to

> Main Street is *parallel to* Lafayette Avenue.

rely on (or *upon*)

> You can *rely on* me to finish what I start.

reminiscent of

> The movie was *reminiscent of* the "good old days."

responsible for

> You are *responsible for* your own actions.

retroactive to (not *from*)

> Your increase will be *retroactive to* January 1.

speak to (tell something to)
speak with (discuss with)

> I will *speak to* the students about this situation.
> If you *speak with* me, we can find a solution.

specialize in

> She will *specialize in* computers and data processing.

talk to (address)
talk with (discuss)

> The visitor *talked to* the audience for an hour.
> I *talked with* my teacher about the problem.

Pronouns

A pronoun is a word used in place of a noun or a name. Its main purpose is to eliminate the need for awkward and monotonous repetition.

The noun that the pronoun replaces is called its *antecedent*. The pronoun must agree with its antecedent in person, number, and gender.

When *Mr. Jones* arrives, please have *him* fill out an application.

When *Mrs. Jones* arrives, please have *her* fill out an application.

When the *applicants* arrive, *they* should first fill out applications.

If you have difficulty mastering the use of pronouns, the chart on the following page should be of value.

The **nominative** case is used (1) when the pronoun is the subject of the sentence, or (2) when it follows any form of the verb *to be* (*be, am, is, are, was, were, been, being, will be, has been*, etc.).

I will call her in the morning. (*I* is the subject.)

We will complete the project tomorrow. (*We* is the subject.)

Is Barbara there? Yes, this is *she*. (*She* follows *is*.)

It was *we* who sponsored the carnival. (*We* follows *was*.)

The **objective** case is used (1) when the pronoun is the object of the verb, or (2) when it is the object of a preposition. An object always answers the question: Whom? What?

They all congratulated *her*. (congratulated whom?)

The doctor gave *him* a prescription. (gave whom?)

Please give *it* to Stan and *me*. (what? to whom?)

Mr. Peterson talked with *them* about the assignment. (with whom?)

The **possessive** case is used to indicate possession, kind, origin, brand, authorship, etc.

The decision is completely *yours*.

That new car has lost *its* shine. (not *it's*)

CASE:	NOMINATIVE		OBJECTIVE		POSSESSIVE	
Number:	Singular	Plural	Singular	Plural	Singular	Plural
First Person	I	we	me	us	my mine	our ours
Second Person	you	you	you	you	your yours	your yours
Third Person (masculine)	he	they	him	them	his	their theirs
Third Person (feminine)	she	they	her	them	her hers	their theirs
Neuter	it	they	it	them	its	their theirs

When using the possessive case, do not add apostrophe *s* (*'s*) because the pronoun itself is already possessive.

> That is *our* book.
> That book is *ours*. (not *our's*)

If you have difficulty with these rules, either complete the sentence mentally or use each pronoun individually. The correct pronoun will then usually be obvious.

> Eric can play the violin better than *I*. (I can)
> They have called as often as *we*. (we have called)
> The attendant stopped Marc and *me* at the gate. (stopped Marc at the gate, stopped me at the gate)
> Do you want *her* or *me*? (Do you want her? Do you want me?)
> *We* secretaries have a very responsible job. (We have)
> Is Bob older or younger than *he*? (than he is)

NOTE: When speaking of another person and yourself, always mention yourself last.

Be certain that your pronoun refers clearly to a definite person, place, or thing. To do so, ask yourself to whom or what the pronoun refers.

> The salesman told Mr. Kraft that *he* does not understand the problem. (*Unclear*: who does not understand the problem? The salesman? Mr. Kraft?)
> Dick Lehnert said that he would like to return to the United States. (*Clear*: "he clearly refers to Dick Lehnert.)

The following pronouns are always singular and take a singular verb and pronouns.

anybody	anything
anyone	each

either	nobody
everybody	nothing
everyone	one
everything	somebody
much	someone
neither	something

Each of these people *is* to be notified.
Everyone has his or *her* own problems.
Neither of Gary's proposals *is* acceptable.

Some one, any one, every one will always be written as two words when the word *of* follows.

Any one of these people will be satisfactory.
If *anyone* calls, I will be in Mr. Barton's office.

The following pronouns are always plural and take a plural verb or pronoun.

both	few	others
many	several	

Both of the congressmen will air *their* views.
Few of the stores *are* closed for the holiday.

The following pronouns may be either singular or plural depending on the antecedent.

all	more	none
any	most	some

All of the *fruit is* finished. (*Fruit* is used as a singular noun.)
None of the *money is* available. (*Money* is used as a singular noun.)
None of the men *are* available. (*Men* is a plural noun.)

WHO AND WHOM

No longer is there any need for confusion! Always use the pronoun *who* when you can substitute the words *he, she,* or *they* for it.

> This company needs a person *who* knows chemistry. (She knows chemistry.)
>
> We always remember people *who* are thoughtful. (He is thoughtful.)
>
> There are many people *who* will not understand. (They will not understand.)

Always use the pronoun *whom* when you can substitute the words *him, her,* or *them* for it.

> To *Whom* This May Concern: (This may concern her.)
>
> Are you the gentleman to *whom* I spoke yesterday? (I spoke to him yesterday.)
>
> Mark Twain is a writer *whom* we will never forget. (We will never forget him.)

The same rule applies to *whoever* and *whomever.*

> Please give me the identity of *whoever* made the donation. (He made the donation.)
>
> I will be delighted to contact *whomever* you recommend. (You recommend them.)

Who and *whom* refer only to people. *That* refers to people, places, and things when introducing essential clauses.

> I need the name of a car dealer *that* has a Citation available.

Which refers to people, places, and things when introducing nonessential clauses.

> The policy *which* we adopted is the best for our situation.

Verbs

The verb is the most important part of the sentence because it expresses an action, a condition, or a state of being. It makes a statement about the subject.

> Mr. Jones *strolls* through the store.
> Mr. Jones *rushed* through the store.
> Mr. Jones *will stroll* through the store.
> Mr. Jones *is rushing* through the store.

The verb tells you whether the action is present, past, in the future, or in progress. The verb tenses are as follows:

present action now happening or in progress

past action was started or has been completed

future action has not yet taken place

present perfect action has been completed, will continue, or may occur again

past perfect action was completed prior to another past action or past time

future perfect action will be completed before a specified time

> I *walk* to school. (present)
> I *walked* to school. (past)
> I *shall walk* to school. (future)
> I *have walked* to school. (present perfect)
> I *had walked* to school. (past perfect)

By tomorrow, I *shall have walked* to school. (future perfect)

When verbs are expressed in the present or past tenses, they are likely to be single words. The remaining tenses, however, require the aid of helping verbs.

The chart on pages 56–57 indicates verb conjugation, with the tenses; first, second, and third persons singular and plural; and the helping verbs.

Not all verbs are regular; that is, they do not have *ed* added to the past and perfect tenses. In irregular verbs either the root of the word changes to indicate past and perfect or it remains the same and no ending is added.

The following list gives proper forms for many irregular verbs.

Present	Past	Perfect
be, am, is, are	was	been
bear	bore	borne
beat	beat	beaten
begin	began	begun
bid (offer price)	bid	bid
bite	bit	bitten
blow	blew	blown
break	broke	broken
bring	brought	brought
build	built	built
burst	burst	burst
buy	bought	bought
catch	caught	caught
choose	chose	chosen
cling	clung	clung
come	came	come
cost	cost	cost

creep	crept	crept
deal	dealt	dealt
dig	dug	dug
drink	drank	drunk
drive	drove	driven
do	did	done
draw	drew	drawn
eat	ate	eaten
fall	fell	fallen
fight	fought	fought
find	found	found
fly	flew	flown
forecast	forecast(ed)	forecast(ed)
forget	forgot	forgotten
freeze	froze	frozen
get	got	got, gotten
give	gave	given
go	went	gone
grind	ground	ground
grow	grew	grown
hang (an object)	hung	hung
hang (a person)	hanged	hanged
have, has	had	had
hit	hit	hit
hurt	hurt	hurt
know	knew	known
lead	led	led
lay (place)	laid	laid
lie (recline)	lay	lain
lie (falsehood)	lied	lied
make	made	made
meet	met	met
pay	paid	paid
prove	proved	proved, proven
put	put	put

quit	quit	quit
raise (lift)	raised	raised
ride	rode	ridden
ring (bell)	rang	rung
rise	rose	risen
run	ran	run
see	saw	seen
seek	sought	sought
sell	sold	sold
set	set	set
shake	shook	shaken
shine (give light)	shone	shone
shine (polish)	shined	shined
show	showed	shown, showed
shrink	shrank	shrunk
sing	sang	sung
sink	sank	sunk
sit (rest)	sat	sat
speak	spoke	spoken
spend	spent	spent
spring	sprang	sprung
steal	stole	stolen
sting	stung	stung
strike	struck	struck, stricken
swear	swore	sworn
swim	swam	swum
swing	swung	swung
take	took	taken
teach	taught	taught
tear	tore	torn
tell	told	told
think	thought	thought
throw	threw	thrown
wear	wore	worn
win	won	won

| wring | wrung | wrung |
| write | wrote | written |

SPECIAL VERB PROBLEMS

1. Two sets of helping verbs that seem to cause difficulty are *can* and *may* and *could* and *might*.

   Can denotes the ability or capacity to do something in the present or future while *could* denotes either the ability or capacity to do something in the past or a future possibility.

   She *can* see you now. (present)
   I *can* arrive early tomorrow. (future)
   Yesterday he *could* not be reached. (past)
   The report *could* be completed in three days. (future)

   May denotes a request for permission or a possibility in the present tense while *might* denotes a request for permission or a possibility in the past or future tenses.

   May we leave early? (Polite request)
   There *might* be a reasonable explanation for their actions.
   We asked if we *might* go.

2. Gerunds are words or phrases that have verbs as the root and *ing* endings. Though formed from verbs they act as nouns. When a gerund is preceded by a noun or a pronoun, the noun or pronoun must take the possessive form.

   I do not like *your calling* me so early in the morning. (*Calling* is a gerund preceded by a possessive pronoun.)
   Bob's constant nagging is annoying. (*Constant nagging* is a gerund phrase preceded by a possessive noun.)

3. The helping verbs *shall* and *will* are commonly confused. *Shall* expresses the future tense when used for the first person, singular and plural. *Will* expresses the future tense when used for the second and third persons, singular and plural.

   I *shall call* you in the morning.
   You *will call* me in the morning.

4. The verb *were* is often used to express wishful thinking or an idea that is contrary to the fact. *Was*, on the other hand, is used to express a statement of fact or possible fact.

   I wish I *were* a millionaire. (wishful thinking)
   She acts as if she *were* president of the company. (contrary to fact)
   If Jack *was* at the airport, I did not see him. (a possible fact)

5. *Should* denotes a duty or an obligation. *Would* denotes a condition or state of being; it is also used to express habitual behavior.

   Our company *should* have the proposal ready by the tenth. (obligation)
   Our company *would* be pleased to have the proposal ready by the tenth. (condition)
   As a boy he *would* always be tinkering with something. (habitual behavior)

6. When using the infinitive form of the verb (the present tense preceded by *to*), do not split the infinitive with a modifier.

Right: The company president wants *to review* the proposal *carefully* before rendering a decision.

Wrong: The company president wants *to carefully review* the proposal before rendering a decision.

Super Stumpers

Lie and *lay*, *sit* and *set*, and *rise* and *raise* are three commonly misused pairs of verbs. They are conjugated as follows:

Present	Past	Perfect
lie	lay	lain
lay	laid	laid
sit	sat	sat
set	set	set
rise	rose	risen
raise	raised	raised

The first verb of each pair (*lie, sit, rise*) does not have an object. In relation to these verbs, you cannot answer the questions: What? Whom? The second verb of each pair (*lay, set, raise*) does have an object. You can answer the questions: What? Whom?

The new building will *lie* between Madison and Fifth avenues. (lie what or whom? not answered)

Please *lay* the book on the desk. (lay what? the book)

I would like to *sit* at the second table. (sit what or whom? not answered)

The man did not know how to *set* the alarm. (set what? the alarm)

The bread will *rise* at a warm temperature. (rise what or whom? not answered)

Raise your glass and toast the new year. (raise what? your glass)

Note that the past tense of *lie* is *lay*, which does not have an object.

Yesterday I was so tired that I *lay* down for an hour.

Subject and Verb Agreement

One of the most basic rules of grammar is that the subject and the verb must agree in number. The third-person singular verb ends in *s*. The plural is the same for all persons.

Third-Person Singular	**All Plurals**
is	are
was	were
has	have
gets	get
tells	tell

The boy *was* there early.
The boys *were* there early.
She *is* aware of the situation.
They *are* aware of the situation.

1. *Many a*, *many an*, and *each and every* always require a singular verb.

    Each and every typewriter *is* needed for the project.
    Many a man *has* been denied the opportunity.

2. *None, some, any, all, most,* and fractions are either singular or plural, depending on the noun they modify.

> *Half* of the *shipment has* been misplaced. (The subject, *shipment,* is singular.)
> *Half* of the *boxes have* been misplaced. (The subject, *boxes,* is plural.)

3. When referring to the name of a book, magazine, song, company, or article, use a singular verb even though the name itself may be plural.

> *Little Women is* one of the great classics.
> *Greenberg & Wanderman is* a fine team of attorneys.

4. When referring to an amount, money, distance, etc., use a singular verb if the noun is thought of as a single unit.

> I feel that $600 *is* a fair price. (a single amount)
> *Six hundred* books *are* located on the shelves. (individual books)

5. For an explanation of collective nouns, refer to the "Nouns" section of this chapter.

6. When *or* or *nor* is used to connect a singular and a plural subject, the verb must agree in number with the person or item closest to the verb.

> Neither the boss nor the *secretaries were* available.
> Neither the secretaries nor the *boss was* available.
> Either Bill or his *sister is* able to attend.
> Either Bill or his *sisters are* able to attend.

	PRESENT	PAST	FUTURE	PRESENT PERFECT	PAST PERFECT	FUTURE PERFECT
I	call	called	shall call	have called	had called	shall have called
you	call	called	will call	have called	had called	will have called
she he it	calls	called	will call	has called	had called	will have called
we	call	called	shall call	have called	had called	shall have called

	PRESENT	PAST	FUTURE	PRESENT PERFECT	PAST PERFECT	FUTURE PERFECT
you	call	called	will call	have called	had called	will have called
they	call	called	will call	have called	had called	will have called

CHAPTER 3

CAPITALIZATION

*First Words, Calendar Dates, Seasons, Holi-
days, Historic Events, Commercial Products,
Compass Points, Diseases, Family Relation-
ships, Governmental Bodies, Heavenly Bodies
and Supreme Beings, Hyphenated Names and
Prefixes, Legal Documents, Literary Titles,
Numbers and Letters with Nouns, Organiza-
tions and Institutions, Personal Names and
Titles, Proper and Common Nouns, School
Subjects*

First Words

1. Always capitalize the first words of (a) a complete sentence, (b) a direct quotation that is a complete sentence,
   and (c) a complete sentence that follows a colon.

   The passenger gave the taxi driver a large tip.
   He said, "Have a wonderful time this evening."
   The sign reads: Keep off the grass.

2. Always capitalize the first word in each line of a poem.

THE LULLABY
The room is shadowed by twilight falling,
And in the silence a voice is calling,
A mother is singing her young one to sleep,
Singing a "lullaby from the deep"...

by Ethel Lorenz

3. Capitalize the major words of the salutation and first word of a complimentary closing of a letter.

Dear Mr. Fredericks: Sincerely yours,
Gentlemen: Very truly yours,
Dear Sir: Yours truly,
Dear Judge Triolo: Respectfully yours,

Calendar Dates, Seasons, Holidays, Historic Events

4. Always capitalize the names of holidays, days of the week, months of the year, historic events, holidays, and specific periods of time.

Thanksgiving   Memorial Day
Wednesday   February
the Renaissance   the McCarthy Era
D-Day   the Civil War

5. Do not capitalize the seasons of the year unless the season is being personified (given human characteristics).

Before Old Man Winter approaches, we should put
on our winter snow tires.

Commercial Products

6. Always capitalize the brand or trade name but not the
noun that it identifies.

Del Monte catsup	Parker pen
Coke	Savarin coffee
Chevrolet automobile	Arrow shirts
Dial soap	Timex watches

7. Do not capitalize terms that derive from proper nouns if
they are no longer associated with their origin and are
used as common nouns.

italian dressing	chauvinist
china (dishes)	french fries
turkish towels	roman numerals
escalator	watt

Compass Points

8. Points on the compass (north, south, east, and west) and
their derivatives are capitalized only when they refer to a
major region, not a direction, or are part of a place name.

I plan to take a trip out West. (major region)
He was traveling east on Route 17 when the accident
occurred. (direction)
Their address is 205 West Maple Avenue. (part of an
address)

I plan to visit the Far East and the Middle East.
(derivatives used for major regions)

9. The adjectives *northern, southern, eastern,* and *western* are
capitalized when they are part of a proper name.

southern Jersey   Eastern Seaboard
Western Hemisphere   Northern Ireland

Diseases

10. Capitalize the name of a disease when it is the name of
an individual.

Parkinson's disease   Hodgkin's disease
measles   virus

Family Relationships

11. Capitalize family titles if they are followed by the person's
name or when used alone as a title.

I am so excited because Uncle Bob and Aunt Elsie
are coming.
I would love for Grandma to knit me a red sweater.

12. Do not capitalize family titles if they are preceded by
possessive pronouns, unless they are followed immediately
by a proper name.

My mother and my uncle had a long conversation.
My mother and my Uncle Ben had a long conversation.

Governmental Bodies and Titles

13. Always capitalize governmental bodies and high-ranking government officials if they are specifically designated.

the Senate	the Supreme Court
the Congress	Federal Bureau of Investigation
the Army	Department of the Interior
the Cabinet	the United Nations

    The President is entertaining a foreign dignitary.

    The Constitution mandates that a presidential candidate must be native born and at least thirty-five years of age.

    This year we will elect a new senator. (not specified)

    The newly elected Senator Smith is currently in Washington. (specific)

Heavenly Bodies and Supreme Beings

14. Always capitalize the names of astronomical bodies such as planets, stars, and constellations. Exceptions are *sun* and *moon*. Names for supreme beings are capitalized, as are many religious terms.

Libra	Allah
God	the Lord
the Bible	Ten Commandments
Earth	the Milky Way

Hyphenated Names and Prefixes

15. Hyphenated names are capitalized as if no hyphen were present.

Spanish-American	Eighty-first Congress
Dallas–Forth Worth	Merriam-Webster
area	dictionaries

16. Hyphenated prefixes are not capitalized, unless the sentence begins with the hyphenated word.

    Ex-President Ford is in Aspen, Colorado.
    We saw *ex*-President Ford in Aspen, Colorado.

Legal Documents

17. In legal documents, the names attributed to the parties are always capitalized.

    The Landlord agrees to supply the Tenant with gas, electricity, and water at no charge to the Tenant.

18. Special introductory phrases, also usually appearing in legal documents, are always in complete capital letters.

    IN WITNESS WHEREOF, the parties...
    KNOW ALL MEN BY THESE PRESENTS:
    WHEREFORE, the undersigned...
    IT IS HEREBY STIPULATED that...

Literary Titles

19. Always capitalize the titles of literary works and articles or chapters appearing within these works. Omit the capitalization of articles, conjunctions, and prepositions unless they start or end the title.

<u>The New York Times</u> or THE NEW YORK TIMES
"How to Winterize Your Home" (article)
<u>Collier's Encyclopedia</u> or COLLIER'S ENCYCLO-
    PEDIA

Books, magazines, newspapers, historical documents, pamphlets, brochures, movies, etc., will be either underscored or in all capital letters. Articles, names of chapters, and other parts within these writings are enclosed in quotation marks.

Numbers and Letters with Nouns

20. Always capitalize a noun that is followed by a number or letter used to identify it. The exceptions are lines, pages, paragraphs, sizes, notes, and verses.

Room 204	page 2
Policy No. 14677868	Appendix A
Catalog No. 25	Lot 3, Tract 123
Invoice No. 1234	size 10
Chapter X	Exhibit A

It is often necessary to use *No.* before the actual number. Do not use the number sign (#) in formal writing.

21. When the noun and the number are separated in the sentence, do not capitalize the descriptive word.

I believe that 204 is the room where the meeting will
    be held.

Organizations and Institutions

22. Always capitalize the major words in the names of insti-
    tutions, banks, colleges, universities, religious bodies,
    schools, hospitals, clubs, political parties, societies, etc.

the Republican party	New York Public Library
the Ford Foundation	the League of Women Voters
the Salvation Army	Congregation Sons of Israel
State University of New York	St. Luke's Hospital

23. Do not capitalize any of the above terms when they are
    used as common nouns.

    In the fall, I will apply to several foundations.
    I must do research at the library.

Personal Names and Titles

24. Capitalize all titles that precede a personal name.

General Eisenhower	Dr. Gorelick
President Jameson	Mayor-elect Smith
Ambassador Jones	Vice-President Sheridan

25. Do not capitalize titles that are used in apposition and are
    set off by commas unless you are referring to a high-ranking
    public dignitary or high-ranking member of your organi-
    zation.

    Mike Fauci, sales representative, is scheduled to re-
    turn to the office tomorrow.

The President of our company, Judy Barash, will preside at the meeting.

26. Treat the spelling of a person's name exactly as the person does. There are instances when a last name may not start with a capital letter or may have an unusual spelling. Check the telephone directory or the person's letterhead.

John Smythe   José deLa Cruz
Evan von Poshe   Ellen and Lucy d'Meglia

Proper and Common Nouns

27. Always capitalize a proper noun (a specific person, place, or thing). Do not capitalize a common noun (a general person, place, or thing).

Common	Proper
state	California
company	International Business Machines
book	GIFTS FROM THE SEA
language	French
holiday	Christmas
school	Taylor Business Institute
building	Empire State Building

I am interested in purchasing the building across the street.
The view from the Chrysler Building is breathtaking.

28. Always capitalize a nickname that commonly substitutes for the real name.

the Bay Area (San Francisco)
the Big Board (New York Stock Exchange)

Big D (Dallas)
the Big Apple (New York City)

29. Always capitalize nationalities and races (with the exception of *black* and *white*).

Caucasian	Afro-American
Indian	Japanese
Eskimo	American

30. Always capitalize the names of continents, nations, states, cities, towns, bodies of water, avenues, harbors, etc.

New York Harbor	Fifth Avenue
New York State	Atlantic Ocean
Hull Township	New England

Do not capitalize a geographical term that precedes a name unless it is a designated part of that name.

I had a wonderful visit to the city of Miami.
New York City has so much to offer.

31. Do not capitalize a plural noun that describes two or more proper nouns.

Meet me at the corner of Main Street and Troy Street.
Meet me at the corner of Main and Troy streets.
I have seen the Appalachian and Rocky mountains.

School Subjects

32. Capitalize the names of courses when they refer to specific courses or are the names of languages.

English	Spanish
Chemistry 201	mathematics
history	History II
Typewriting 102	Introduction to Shorthand

CHAPTER 4

NUMBERS

Basic Rules, Addresses, Adjacent Numbers, Ages and Anniversaries, Amounts of Money, Beginning Sentences, Book Divisions, Centuries and Decades, Dates, Decimals, Dimensions, Degrees, Quotations, Fractions and Mixed Numbers, Hours of the Day, Hyphenated Numbers, Ordinals, Millions and Above, Percentages, Roman Numerals, Weights and Measures, One Final Note

Basic Rules

1. Numbers from one to ten are generally written as words, and numbers above ten are generally written as figures. This rule applies to exact numbers and approximations.

   Only five people volunteered to help.
   There were 20 people who volunteered to help.
   Approximately 50,000 tickets were sold for the concert.
   About ten cartons should be sufficient.

2. Numbers in a sentence that perform the same function should be written uniformly. If one is written as a figure, all should be expressed as figures.

We completed only 9 of the 12 projects.
We ordered 3 desks, 3 chairs, and 15 lighting fixtures.
She bought four 75-watt bulbs. (different functions)

Addresses

3. Use figures to represent a house or building number, with the exception of *one*, which should be spelled out.

   He resides at One Park Place.
   He resides at 2 Park Place.

4. Street numbers from one to ten should be written as words, and street numbers above ten should be written as figures. Most writers omit the *st*, *nd*, and *th* endings after the numbers.

   He resides at 205 *Second* Avenue.
   He resides at 205 - 14 Street.

   When the house number and street address are both written as figures, separate them with a hyphen leaving a space on either side of the hyphen. This avoids misreading.

5. ZIP code numbers are written as figures, one space after the two-letter state abbreviation (if in an inside address) and one space after the full state name (if in sentence form).

   Mr. and Mrs. Robert Hersch
   52 Northampton C - Century Village
   West Palm Beach, FL 33409

Mr. and Mrs. Robert Hersch reside at 52 Northampton C - Century Village, West Palm Beach, Florida 33409.

Adjacent Numbers

6. When two unrelated numbers are written together, generally write one as figures and the other as words. The one in words should be the shorter of the two. If both are too large to be written in words, write both as figures and use a comma to separate them. If both are written as words, also use a comma to separate them.

   We had two $100 bills.
   The landlord owns two 6-room homes.
   In 1970, 315 of the company's employees moved to Atlanta.
   Of the three, two qualified.

Ages and Anniversaries

7. Ages are generally written as words unless they represent a significant statistic.

   Our company has a mandatory retirement age of 65. (significant)
   Mr. Smith will be forty-nine on his next birthday. (not significant)

8. When ages are expressed in years, months, and days, they are generally written as figures with no comma separation.

   The little boy is 2 years 1 month and 4 days old.

Amounts of Money

9. Figures are used to represent exact amounts of money. The dollar sign ($) is placed immediately before the number and no ciphers (.00) are used when expressing even dollar amounts.

   A balance of $350.50 remains in our treasury.
   A balance of $350 remains in our treasury.

10. In a column, add the ciphers to all amounts if *any* number in that column contains cents.

   $150.00
    50.50
    200.00
   $400.50

11. For amounts less than a dollar, the word *cents* follows the number. The cents symbol (¢) is used when referring to invoices, purchase orders, or technical or statistical quotations.

   He received only 45 cents in change.
   Yesterday's market showed a gain of 35¢ and 75¢ on the stocks we had discussed.

12. Indefinite amounts of money are generally spelled out.

   A few million dollars will be needed to complete the project.
   Many hundreds of dollars need to be raised by June.

13. For uniformity and clarity, use the dollar sign with amounts under a dollar in a series of related numbers when dollars and cents are mixed.

The young child received the following amounts of money by selling lemonade: $1.50, $2.00, and $.95.

14. Money representing a million dollars or more should be expressed as follows:

A $3.5 million budget has recently been approved.

15. If the million dollar figure consists of more than a whole number and simple fractional amount, use figures.

The company realized a profit of $3,245,000 last year.

Beginning Sentences

16. When a number begins a sentence, the number must be written as words. If the number is too long, it may be necessary to reword the sentence.

Right: Thirty-five people were injured in the fire.
Wrong: 35 people were injured in the fire.
Right: In 1979 we had our best year.
Wrong: 1979 was our best year.

Book Divisions

17. Pages and divisions of a book are referred to in figures. For capitalization, see Rule 20 of the "Capitalization" chapter.

The information appears in Volume X, Chapter 3, page 3, line 2 of the book we just discussed.

Centuries and Decades

18. Centuries and decades may be expressed in either of the
    styles shown below. Decades are not capitalized except in
    such expressions as the *Roaring Twenties* or the *Gay Nine-
    ties*.

    Our company was founded in the early 1900s. (1900's)
    Our company was founded in the early nineteen
        hundreds.
    The twentieth century has shown more progress than
        any other.

Dates

19. When the day follows the month, use figures only.

    The meeting was tentatively scheduled for May 1,
        1983.
    The draft must be submitted no later than June 1.
        (not *June 1st* or *June first*)

NOTE: Check "Addresses and Dates" in the comma section
of the "Punctuation" chapter for comma rules governing dates.

20. When the day stands alone or precedes the month, it may
    be expressed in ordinal figures or in ordinal words, de-
    pending on the degree of emphasis indicated.

    The meeting is tentatively scheduled for the 1st of
        May.
    The meeting is tentatively scheduled for the first of
        May.
    I plan to arrive on the tenth; can you meet me?

In formal writing, always spell out the names of months. (not *Mar. 1, 1977* or *3/1/77*)

21. In military or foreign correspondence the date is frequently written as follows:

    22 September 1979

22. In very formal documents, both the day and the year are spelled out.

    on the sixteenth of September, in the year of Our Lord one thousand nine hundred eighty-two
    on the sixteenth of September, one thousand nine hundred eighty-two (or *and eighty-two*)

Decimals, Dimensions, Degrees, Quotations

23. Decimals are always written as figures with no comma separation to the right of the decimal.

    25.5678 (no comma separation to the right)
    8,543.5678 (comma separation to the left)

24. Dimensions are always written as figures in either of the following ways:

    The rug measures 9 by 12 feet.
    The rug measures 9 × 12 feet.

25. Degrees are always written as figures with either the word *degree* or the degree symbol (°).

The temperature is a blustery 22 degrees below zero.
The temperature is a blustery 22° below zero.

26. Stock market quotations are always written as figures.

    The common stock we discussed closed at 79½.

Fractions and Mixed Numbers

27. Fractions not expressed with whole numbers are written
    as words.

    By the time I arrived home, three-fourths of the pie
        had been eaten. (Always separate the numerator
        from the denominator with a hyphen.)

28. Fractions expressed with whole numbers are written as
    figures.

    The runner had to complete an additional 3-3/4 miles
        in order to win the race.

    A fraction that does not appear on your keyboard can be
    formed by using the diagonal, as above.

Hours of the Day

29. Hours of the day are expressed as figures when *a.m.* or
    p.m. (AM or PM) follow. When no minutes are indicated,
    the ciphers (:00) should not be used.

                 My train will arrive at 9:15 a.m.
                 My train will arrive at 9 p.m.

The ciphers should be used, however, to create uniformity in related hours.

My train will arrive between 9:00 and 9:15 p.m.

30. When the hours of the day are not followed by a.m. or p.m. but by the word *o'clock*, either figures or words may be used.

ten o'clock   10 o'clock

31. The words *noon* and *midnight* are used to express the 12 o'clock hours.

I can meet you for lunch at 12 noon.
I must arrive home no later than 12 midnight.

Hyphenated Numbers

32. The compound numbers 21 to 99 are always hyphenated when written as words.

Twenty-one people attended the party.
One hundred fifty-two people attended the party.

33. A hyphen may be used to represent numbers in a continuous series.

Please read pages 205-215.
He served one term, 1976-1979. (not *from 1976-1979*)

Ordinals

34. Ordinals can be used as words or figures depending on the related rules and degree of emphasis.

Join us for our 50th anniversary sale! (emphasis)
This is our second year in business. (no emphasis)

35. Ordinal figures are expressed in any of the following ways
with no period following.

Thomas James Lindsell 2nd
Thomas James Lindsell 2d
Thomas James Lindsell II
Thomas James Lindsell, Jr. (When *Jr.* is used in place
of the ordinal, a comma precedes it.)

Millions and Above

36. Any number of a million or more is treated as indicated
for money amounts in Rules 15 and 16.

The winner of the congressional race received more
than 2.5 million votes.
The candidate received 2,560,000 votes.

Percentages

37. Percentages are written as figures followed by the word
percent unless beginning a sentence.

Only 25 percent of the votes were counted.
Twenty-five percent of the votes were counted.

38. Fractional percentages may be expressed as follows:

one-fourth of one percent   .25 percent

39. When a hyphen is used to connect percentages, the word *percent* should be placed after the last amount. When the percent symbol (%) is used, it must follow each figure. (The percent symbol is used in invoices, tabulations, etc.)

The candidate received only 25–30 percent of the votes.

The invoice indicated a 2% or 3% discount, depending on the promptness of payment.

Roman Numerals

40. Roman numerals are used as divisions of literary works, legislative material, topics of outlines, dates on public buildings, etc. When used for any of the above, they will always be in capital letters. When used to indicate pages in the foreword or preface of a book, small roman numerals are used.

1 I	16 XVI	400 CD
2 II	19 XIX	500 D
3 III	20 XX	600 DC
4 IV	21 XXI	700 DCC
5 V	25 XXV	800 DCCC
6 VI	30 XXX	900 CM
7 VII	40 XL	1000 M
8 VIII	50 L	1100 MC
9 IX	60 LX	1200 MCC
10 X	70 LXX	1300 MCCC
11 XI	80 LXXX	1400 MCD
12 XII	90 XC	1500 MD
13 XIII	100 C	1600 MDC
14 XIV	200 CC	1700 MDCC
15 XV	300 CCC	1800 MDCCC

1900 MCM	3000 MMM
2000 MM	1984 MCMLXXXIV

pages in a *foreword or preface*: i, ii, iii, iv, etc.

Weights and Measures

41. Dimensions, weights, distances, measurements, etc. should be written as figures followed by the spelled-out version of the unit or measurement.

    The basketball player stood 7 feet 5 inches tall.
    The package weighs 5 pounds 10 ounces.

    Note that no commas are used to separate these units.

One Final Note

Numbers listed in a column should always be justified (lined up) at the right.

$$
\begin{array}{r}
200 \\
1,500 \\
6 \\
17,567 \\
25
\end{array}
$$

CHAPTER 5

WORD DIVISION

A word divided incorrectly is a misspelled word. Consult your dictionary when in doubt, and adhere to the following rules.

DON'TS

1. Do not use excessive word division.
2. Do not divide a word in the first line or last line on a page.
3. Do not divide a word in the first line of a paragraph.
4. Do not divide a one-syllable word, no matter how long the word may be. (*length, brought, straight*)
5. Do not divide words on two consecutive lines.
6. Do not divide a proper name or number. (*Washington, $153.69*)
7. Do not separate one or two letters from the rest of the word. (*acute, overall, reward, heater, shovel*)
8. Do not separate contractions or abbreviations. (*shouldn't, NATO, ASPCA*)

DO'S

1. A word should be divided only between syllables. Dic-

tionaries indicate syllabication by the use of a bold •, but rely on your rules also.

com•fort	pro•ce•dure

2. A word should be divided only if it contains six letters or more.

inept	pre•pare
bugle	tar•nish

3. If a vowel stands alone as a single syllable, it must remain on the same line as the first part of the word.

experi•ment	mini•mum
obitu•ary	initia•tive

4. A word will generally be divided between double consonants.

admis•sion	bat•tery
cud•dle	neces•sary

Exception: Do not divide a word between double consonants if it means breaking up the root of the word.

pass•ing	install•ing
call•ers	process•ing

5. If a word contains a natural hyphen, divide only at that point.

self-determination (Hyphenate words starting with *self*, except *selfish* and *selfless*.)

two-thirds

fifty-six

6. If a word contains a prefix or suffix, it is best to divide at that point.

> establish•ment   dis•appear
> draw•ing   pre•determine

CHAPTER 6

SPELLING

Doubling the Final Consonants, The Final e, The Final y, ie and ei, Plurals, Prefixes, Suffixes

Spelling Motto: *If in doubt, check it out!*

The common outcry of employers is "My secretary cannot spell." If you produce a masterpiece of typing and it contains a spelling error, what do you think will be remembered? Your error.

Your dictionary can be one of your most valuable reference guides, but you should make a list of words with which you have difficulty and which are used frequently in your particular company or industry. Don't waste time constantly checking your dictionary; your own word list together with a knowledge of the rules of spelling will aid you in overcoming many of the spelling difficulties you may have.

NOTE: There are exceptions to every rule.

Doubling the Final Consonant

Double the final consonant before a suffix if:
1. It is a one-syllable word or has its accent on the last syllable.

hop	hopped	hopping
commit	committed	committing
plan	planned	planning
defer	deferred	deferring
omit	omitted	omitting

2. It is a word ending in a single vowel followed by a single consonant.

occur	occurred	occurring
transfer	transferred	transferring
prefer	preferred	preferring
infer	inferred	inferring
permit	permitted	permitting
allot	allotted	allotting

The Final e

Drop the final *e* preceded by a consonant before a suffix that starts with a vowel.

excuse + able = excusable
like + able = likable
obese + ity = obesity
entitle + ing = entitling
argue + ing = arguing
desire + ous = desirous
(Common exceptions: changeable, noticeable, courageous)

Retain the final *e* when the suffix begins with a consonant.

move + ment = movement
strange + ly = strangely

appropriate + ly = appropriately
state + ment = statement
care + less = careless
resource + ful = resourceful

The Final y

Retain the final y when it is preceded by a vowel.

attorney + s = attorneys
annoy + ed = annoyed
buy + er = buyer
journey + s = journeys
employ + ers = employers
annoy + ance = annoyance

Change the final y to an *i* when it is preceded by a consonant.

salary + es = salaries
reply + ed = replied
beauty + ful = beautiful
angry + ly = angrily
cozy + ness = coziness
easy + ly = easily

ie and ei

Put *i* before *e*, (fiend, yield)
Except after *c*, (receive, conceit)
Or when sounded like *a*,
As in *neighbor* and *weigh*;

And except *seize* and *seizure*,
And also *leisure*,
Weird, height, and *either,*
Forfeit and *neither.*

handkerchief	deceit
client	surveillance
niece	heir

Plurals

The plurals of most nouns are formed by the addition of *s*.

    cat + s = cats
    automobile + s = automobiles
    hand + s = hands
    typewriter + s = typewriters
    tree + s = trees
    employee + s = employees

Words ending in *s, x, z, ch,* or *sh* are made plural by the addition of *es*.

    business + es = businesses
    catch + es = catches
    Jones + es = Joneses
    Sanchez + es = Sanchezes
    tax + es = taxes
    box + es = boxes

Words ending in *y* that are preceded by a vowel are made plural by the addition of an *s*.

    key + s = keys
    journey + s = journeys

alley + s = alleys
turkey + s = turkeys
attorney + s = attorneys
chimney + s = chimneys

Words ending in y that are preceded by a consonant are made plural by changing the y to i and adding es.

academy + es = academies
secretary + es = secretaries
company + es = companies
cry + es = cries
army + es = armies
beneficiary + es = beneficiaries

Exception: When a person's name ends in y and is preceded by a consonant, it is made plural by the addition of an s. Otherwise it would be unclear, in some cases, whether the name ends in y or i.

Kennedy + s = Kennedys
Mary + s = Marys
Pokarsky + s = Pokarskys

Words ending in o that are preceded by a vowel are generally made plural by the addition of an s.

studio + s = studios
radio + s = radios

Most words ending in o that are preceded by a consonant are made plural by the addition of es; however, some require only an s. If in doubt, check it out!

veto + es = vetoes
echo + es = echoes
hero + es = heroes

Musical terms ending in *o* are made plural by the addition of an *s*.

```
piano + s = pianos
soprano + s = sopranos
banjo + s = banjos
solo + s = solos
```

Some words are made plural by changing the vowel and/or the form.

man	men
mouse	mice
child	children
tooth	teeth
Mr.	Messrs. (from French)
Mrs.	Mmes. (from French)
ox	oxen

Some words are the same in the singular and plural forms.

deer	deer
news	news
mathematics	mathematics
economics	economics
series	series
sheep	sheep

In a hyphenated compound word, the principal part of the word will be made plural.

brother-in-law	brothers-in-law
sister-in-law	sisters-in-law
editor-in-chief	editors-in-chief

In a compound word that is not hyphenated, the *s* is added at the end.

cupful	cupfuls
handful	handfuls
letterhead	letterheads

Some words that end in *f* or *fe* are made plural by changing the *f* to a *v* and adding *s* or *es*.
*Again, if in doubt, check it out.

staff + s = staffs
belief + s = beliefs
roof + s = roofs
brief + s = briefs
knife + s = knives
shelf + s = shelves
life + s = lives
wife + s = wives

Letters, signs, and figures are made plural by the addition of apostrophe *s*.

Always dot your *i*'s and cross your *t*'s.
Your 6's are not too clear; they look like O's.
Four R.N.'s applied for the nursing position.

A contraction is made plural by the addition of an *s*.

don'ts   can'ts

Many borrowed foreign words are made plural by changing the ending.

sis to *ses*:	analysis	analyses
	crisis	crises
	oasis	oases
um to *a*:	datum	data
	addendum	addenda
	memorandum	memoranda (memorandums)

us to *i*:	stimulus	stimuli
	cactus	cacti
	radius	radii
on to *a*:	criterion	criteria
	phenomenon	phenomena
	automaton	automata

Prefixes

The understanding of words is the key to opening doors and expanding minds. You can greatly increase your vocabulary if you are familiar with the meanings of commonly used prefixes. A prefix is a letter or letters attached to the beginning of a root word to change its meaning.

Prefix	Meaning	Example
a-	not	amoral, atypical
ante-	before	antecedent, anteroom
anti-	against	anti-American, antifreeze
arch-	chief	archbishop, archrival
auto-	self	autobiography, automobile (self-moving)
bi-	two	biannually, bicycle
circum-	around	circumstance, circumvent
com-	together	combine, common
con-	with	confer, contact
contra-	against	contradict, contraception
de-	away from	depart, decrease

dis-	opposite of	dissatisfy, dishonest
em-	cause	employ, empathy
en-	cause	enable, enlist
epi-	above, upon	epidermis, epidemic
ex-	former, out	ex-President, exit
for-	away	forgive, forward
fore-	before	forearm, foreground
hyper-	above	hyperactive, hyperbole
hypo-	under	hypodermic, hypocrite
inter-	between	interstate, interact
intra-	inside	intrastate, intramural
intro-	inside	introduce, introvert
ir-	not	irresponsible, irregular
mis-	wrong	mismanagement, misconception
mono-	one	monogamous, monopoly
non-	not	nonessential, nonsense
para-	near	paramedic, paraphrase
per-	thorough, thoroughly	perceive, perfect
peri-	around	perimeter, periscope
post-	after	postpone, postscript (P.S.)
pre-	before	prearrange, precaution
pro-	for, forward	pro-American, promote
pseudo-	false	pseudonym, pseudo-pregnancy
re-	again	repay, redirect
retro-	backward	retroactive, retrogress
sub-	below	substitute, submarine
super-	above	supervise, superficial
trans-	across	transaction, transfer
un-	not	unpopular, unnecessary

Suffixes

A suffix is a letter or letters added to the end of a word. Suffixes give additional information, change the part of speech, or both. If a suffix has more than one spelling (*sion* and *tion*, *ible* and *able*, *ance* and *ence*), there is no definite rule for choosing between commonly confused spellings. Remember the motto: If in doubt, check it out.

Suffix	Meaning	Example
-able, -ible	able to	comfortable, accessible
-age	condition of	storage, postage
-al	like	fictional, occasional
-an	native of, skilled in	American, historian
-ance, -ence	state of	performance, occurrence
-ary, -ery, -ory	place of	infirmary, bindery, armory
-cy	state of	bankruptcy, accuracy
-dom	position	kingdom, freedom
-ed	past tense	happened, confused
-ee	object of action	employee, addressee
-en	become	heighten, sharpen
-er, -or	person who	mortgagor, rancher
-ese	language	Japanese, legalese
-est	most	largest, happiest
-ful	full of	eventful, harmful
-hood	state of	childhood, neighborhood
-ic, -ical	containing, characterized by	alcoholic, comic, economical, practical
-ine	like	canine, equine

-ing	act in progress	running, standing
-ion, -sion, -tion	process of	description, explosion
-ish	like, of	childish, Finnish
-ism	practice of	Buddhism, alcoholism
-ist	person who	columnist, pianist
-ite	native of, follower	Israelite, favorite
-itis	inflammation	phlebitis, appendicitis
-ity	condition	sincerity, possibility
-ive	having to do with	possessive, passive
-ize, -ise, -yze	become	terrorize, paralyze
-less	without	careless, fearless
-let	small	pamphlet, booklet
-ly	manner, degree	northerly, quickly
-ment	state of	movement, entertainment
-most	greatest	foremost, uttermost
-ness	state of	kindness, happiness
-ology	study of	psychology, terminology
-ous	nature of	famous, religious
-ship	status	citizenship, friendship
-some	tending to	troublesome, lonesome
-ure	act of, agent	failure, legislature
-ward	leading to	toward, forward
-wise	manner of	likewise, clockwise

CHAPTER 7

201 COMMONLY MISSPELLED WORDS

abbreviation
absence
absorption
accept
accessible
accommodate
accompanied
acknowledge
acquaintance
across
advantageous
affect
affiliated
a lot
already
ambiguity
among
analysis
anonymous
apparent
appearance
appreciate

appropriate
argument
arrangement
attendance
bankruptcy
beginning
believable
beneficial
benefited
bookkeeping
bulletin
business
calendar
campaign
cancel
cannot
category
cemetery
changeable
clientele
coming
committee

competition
concede
confident
conscientious
controversy
convenience
convenient
corroborate
criticism
defendant
depreciate
description
desirable
difference
disappoint
disbursement
discrepancy
dissatisfactory
dissipate
effect
eligible
embarrass

endeavor
endorsement
enthusiastic
environment
equipped
especially
exceed
excellent
except
exercise
exhaust
existence
experience
explanation
extension
extraordinary
familiar
feasible
February
foreign
forty
fourth
government
grateful
guarantee
handwritten
height
immediately
inasmuch as
incidentally
independence
independent
indispensable
insistent

interpret
its
jeopardize
jewelry
judgment
knowledge
laboratory
leisure
license
lien
likable
litigation
loose
lose
maintenance
mandatory
mediocre
mileage
minimum
miscellaneous
misspelling
municipal
necessary
oblige
occasion
occurred
occurrence
omission
omitted
opportunity
opposite
original
overdue
paid

pamphlet
parallel
paralyze
perseverance
personal
personnel
persuade
photostat
physician
possession
practical
practically
precede
predictable
preferred
principal
principle
privilege
probably
procedure
proceed
professor
prosecute
psychology
pursue
quantity
questionnaire
really
receive
reciprocal
recommend
reference
referred
referring

repetition	strictly	unanimous
requirement	subpoena	undoubtedly
restaurant	succeed	unnecessary
schedule	successful	until
secretary	surprise	using
separate	sympathy	vacuum
sheriff	techniques	volume
similar	their	weather
sincerely	there	Wednesday
stationary	too	whether
stationery	truly	withheld

CHAPTER 8

COMMONLY CONFUSED WORDS

accede (v)	to yield, assent
exceed (v)	to surpass or go beyond

The smaller nation will *accede* to the conquering larger nation.

He *exceeded* all expectations.

accept (v)	to take or receive
except (prep)	other than

Please *accept* my apology.

No one will understand *except* Thomas.

access (n)	right to enter, admittance
assess (v)	set a value
excess (n)	extra or surplus
(adj)	extra or surplus

Please grant Mr. Feiler *access* to the files.

We will *assess* the situation at a later date.

This *excess* in spending can no longer be tolerated.

The *excess* paper will be collected tomorrow.

ad (n)	short for *advertisement*
add (v)	to increase, unite, or combine

I saw your *ad* in yesterday's newspaper.
Please *add* this book to your collection.

adapt (v)	to adjust, make fit
adept (adj)	skilled or expert at
adopt (v)	take as your own, accept, choose

You must learn to *adapt* to various climates.
He is a highly *adept* swimmer.
The corporation will *adopt* new bylaws.

addenda (n)	(plural of *addendum*) something added
agenda (n)	program of things to be done

The attorney added two *addenda* to the contract.
Please put Mr. Teisch on the *agenda* for tomorrow.

addition (n)	something added
edition (n)	published work

Janice is a welcome *addition* to our staff.
The new *edition* will be published next month.

adverse (adj)	hostile, opposite in direction, unfavorable
averse (adj)	unwilling, disinclined

The *adverse* weather conditions caused many hardships.
I would not be *averse* to your suggestions.

advice (n)	an opinion, counsel, recommendation
advise (v)	to give an opinion, to counsel

This is very sound *advice*.
Please *advise* me if the situation changes.

affect (v)	to influence
effect (n)	result
(v)	to bring about, accomplish

Your attitude will *affect* your performance.
What *effect* did Mr. Sullivan's actions have on you?
You can *effect* many changes if you persevere.

air (n)	atmosphere
heir (n)	person who inherits

The *air* quality today is favorable.
The *heir* to the estate is Jackie Lorenz.

aisle (n)	passageway
isle (n)	island
I'll (contraction)	I shall

The *aisles* in the theater are very narrow.
The British *Isles* are very beautiful.
I'll see you tomorrow evening.

allowed (v)	past tense of *allow*
aloud (adv)	loudly, audibly

They will be *allowed* to tour the factory tomorrow.
Please speak *aloud*.

allusion (n)	indirect reference, casual mention
illusion (n)	false idea or impression
elusion (n)	escape, avoidance
delusion (n)	false belief

His *allusion* to their meeting was unintentional.
An optical *illusion* was created by the mirror.
His *elusion* of the police baffled everyone.
Napoleon suffered from *delusions* of grandeur.

already (adv/adj)	previously
all ready* (adj)	all prepared

We were *already* introduced.
The children were *all ready* for their test.

alright	nonstandard English for *all right*
all right	entirely correct

Will it be *all right* to make the delivery in June?
Are you *all right*?

altar (n)	part of church, raised platform
alter (v)	to change

The bride and groom were married in front of the
   altar.
Do not *alter* your plans on my behalf.

alternate (v)	to substitute or take turns
(n)	a substitute
alternative (n)	one of two or more options

Please *alternate* between the odd and the even.
An *alternate* will be selected in case of illness.
Several *alternatives* must be considered.

altogether (adv)	entirely
all together* (adv)	everyone in one group

He is *altogether* too tall to be a jockey.
The family was *all together* for the reading of the will.

When the word *all* can be omitted and the sentence still makes sense, it will be the two-word version.
The papers are (*all*) *together* on my desk.

annual (adj)	yearly
annul (v)	to cancel

This magazine is an *annual* publication.
Mr. and Mrs. Feiler will not *annul* their marriage.

ante- (prefix)	before
anti- (prefix)	against

The *ante*room was beautifully decorated.
The *anti*biotic should help fight the disease.

appraise (v)	estimate or set value on
apprise (v)	notify, inform

The property was *appraised* at $40,000.
Kindly *apprise* me if his condition worsens.

are (v)	form of verb *to be*
hour (n)	period of time
our (adj)	belonging to us

There *are* many people who will believe her story.
Sam Barash seems to be busy every *hour* in the day.
Our possessions are of great value.

area (n)	place, surface, scope
aria (n)	melody
arrears (n)	being behind in obligation

The entire *area* was muddy after the rain.
The *aria* was beautifully sung.
His account is 30 days in *arrears*.

arraign (v)   to accuse, bring to court
arrange (v)   ⟩   to put in order

    The accused was *arraigned* on charges of reckless driving.
    Please *arrange* the files in numerical order.

ascent (n)   the act of rising or climbing
assent (n)   consent
   (v)   to agree to

    The mountain climber found the *ascent* to be difficult.
    The *assent* was given by the judge.
    The judge *assented* to the decision of the jury.

assistance (n)   help, aid
assistants (n)   those who help

    Any *assistance* will be greatly appreciated.
    Two *assistants* volunteered to move the furniture.

attendance (n)   act of attending, total number attending
attendants (n)   persons who attend

    Your *attendance* in class is required.
    The parking lot *attendants* were most helpful.

aural (adj)   relating to the ear
oral (adj)   relating to the mouth

    The *aural* infection caused his ear to swell.
    The dentist performed an *oral* examination.

bail (n)	security, release
(v)	to set free, to deliver in trust
bale (n)	a bundle

Bail was arranged for the prisoner.
He was *bailed* out of jail.
A *bale* of hay lasts only a short time.

bare (adj)	naked, no more than
bear (v)	to carry, to endure, to produce
(n)	animal

These are the *bare* facts.
She could not *bear* to leave him home.
The *bear* is shedding its fur.

base (n)	foundation
(adj)	lacking decency
bass (n)	species of fish, lowest male voice

The *base* of the building is concrete.
Because of his *base* personality, people avoided him.
They fished for *bass*.
His *bass* voice enhances the choir.

| bases (n) | plural of *base* and *basis* |
| basis (n) | foundation, main factor |

The decision was made on the *bases* of input from
both of you.
There is no solid *basis* for your decision.

| bazaar (n) | marketplace |
| bizarre (adj) | odd, queer |

The *bazaar* offered many bargains.
What a *bizarre* ending to that story.

beat (n)   tempo, series of movements
beet (n)   vegetable

> The *beat* of that music is good for dancing.
> The *beet* crop did not do very well with all the rain
>   we had.

berry (n)   small, juicy fruit
bury (v)   to hide, cover over

> The *berry* had a delicious flavor.
> Let's *bury* our problems and go forward.

beside (prep)   near, alongside
besides (prep)   in addition to

> The plant was placed *beside* the table.
> The man has two dogs *besides* Rusty.

better (adj)   comparative degree of *good*
bettor (n)   person who gambles

> The apple was *better* than the pear.
> The *bettor* is not always the winner.

biannual (adj)   twice a year, semiannual
biennial (adj)   every two years

> Prepare for the *biannual* meeting of the board of di-
>   rectors.
> A *biennial* planting should be sufficient.

bibliography (n)   list of sources of information
biography (n)   account of a person's life

> The *bibliography* will be found at the end of the book.
> Roosevelt's *biography* was of great interest to me.

| birth (n) | act of bringing forth |
| berth (n) | a bed |

The *birth* of their child was a great joy.

I believe the lower *berth* is reserved.

board (n)	plank, counsel, regular meals
(v)	close up with planks, provide meals
bored (v)	penetrated, as with a drill
(adj)	uninterested, wearied from tedium

The *Board* will meet to discuss the new proposal.

Room and *board* will be provided at no additional charge.

After they had *bored* through the wall, they had ventilation.

Marc was *bored* at the meeting; therefore, he left early.

| boarder (n) | one who pays for meals and lodging |
| border (n) | edge or margin |

Our *boarder* will be gone during the month of July.

The *border* on the glass is gold.

| bolder (adj) | more bold or daring |
| boulder (n) | large rock |

Eric is *bolder* than I will ever be.

The large *boulder* was impossible to move manually.

| born | past participle of *bear*, brought forth |
| borne | past participle of *bear*, carried, endured |

The child was *born* on August 15.

Jonathan has *borne* many problems during the year.

| boy (n) | male child |
| buoy (n) | a floating marker |

Michael Gasparre is the *boy* I have been telling you about.

Quickly, grab the *buoy*, and you will stay afloat.

brake (n)	device for stopping motion
(v)	to stop by using a brake
break (n)	a breach, fracture, sudden move
(v)	to breach, fracture, or divide

The *brake* is to the left of the gas pedal.

If you *brake* on ice, you may skid.

The accused made a sudden *break* for the door.

If you *break* the contract, you will be sued.

| bread (n) | food made of dough |
| bred | past participle of *breed*, brought up |

Rye *bread* is my favorite.

David Dworkin is a well-*bred* young man.

bridal (adj)	of a bride or wedding
bridle (n)	harness for a horse
(v)	to restrain

The *bridal* party was dressed in lilac.

The horse pulled at his *bridle*.

Some gossips would be wise to *bridle* their tongues.

| broach (v) | to bring up, introduce |
| brooch (n) | ornamental piece of jewelry |

I would not *broach* the subject until later.

Mrs. Teisch's *brooch* is exquisite.

build (v)   erect or construct
billed   past participle of *bill*, to charge

> Mr. Sheridan will *build* his store on this site.
> You will not be *billed* for the merchandise until next
>   month.

buy (v)   to purchase
by (prep)   expressing relationship of space, time,
                           mode

> We have become a *buy*-now-and-pay-later society.
> Please have the project completed *by* noon.

calendar (n)   a record of time
calender (n)   machine for processing cloth or paper

> I must get a *calendar* for the new year.
> The order will be delayed because the *calender* is in
>   need of repair.

cannot   correct form for *can not*

> I *cannot* see any purpose in continuing this discussion.

canvas (n)   a coarse cloth
canvass (v)   to solicit

> The sailor's duffel bag was made of *canvas*.
> Politicians *canvass* neighborhoods seeking votes.

capital (n)   official city of a state, money, wealth
capital (adj)   chief, serious
capitol (n)   building which houses a state legisla-
                           ture

Capitol (n)   building in Washington, DC which
                            houses Congress

Much *capital* will be needed to start a business.
Murder is a *capital* offense.
The *capitol* in Albany is in need of repair.
When in Washington, do not miss seeing the *Capitol*.

carton (n)   cardboard or wooden box
cartoon (n)   a caricature

The large *carton* will be stored in the attic.
The *cartoon* was very funny.

casual (adj)   not planned, random
causal (adj)   pertaining to a cause

His style is extremely *casual*.
One *causal* factor of the explosion was human error.

cease (v)   to stop
seize (v)   to grasp

You are to *cease* making that noise.
The man was *seized* in the restaurant.

cede (v)   to grant, surrender
seed (n)   that from which something is grown

We are going to *cede* the adjoining property to our
    neighbor.
The *seeds* will be ready for planting in the spring.

ceiling (n)   top of a room or limit
sealing (gerund)   act of closing

The *ceiling* will be set at $2 million.
Sealing the surface will prevent leakage.

census (n)	official counting
senses (n)	(plural) feelings, reaction to stimuli
(v)	perceives, comprehends

The *census* tells of population trends.
Of all our *senses*, sight is the most acute.
The woman *senses* that something may be wrong.

cent (n)	a penny
scent (n)	odor or smell
sent (v)	past tense of *send*, dispatched

Jason spent every *cent* on the gift for his mother.
Garlic leaves a very strong *scent*.
The messenger was *sent* for the package.

cereal (n)	any grain food
serial (adj)	in a series

Adam Rosen's favorite *cereal* is oatmeal.
You must supply us with your *serial* number.

choose (v)	to select
chose (v)	past tense of *choose*
chews (v)	masticates, grinds with teeth

The committee must *choose* a chairperson no later
    than tomorrow.
The accused *chose* to remain silent.
She *chews* gum, and it is not very flattering.

chord (n)	a pleasant combination of tones
cord (n)	string or rope, measurement of wood

The boy could play only one *chord* on his guitar.
The *cord* of wood could not be tied with *cord*.

cite (v)	to summon or make reference to
sight (n)	that which is seen, act of seeing
site (n)	location

You must *cite* an example to prove your point.
The man caught *sight* of the blue car as it went by.
The *site* for our new building has not been determined.

clothes (n)	wearing apparel
cloths (n)	fabrics
close (v)	to terminate
(n)	the end

The *clothes* went on sale after the holiday.
The *cloths* were all imported.
We must *close* the deal by Monday morning.
She left at the *close* of the meeting.

coarse (adj)	rough, common
course (n)	direction, action, part of a meal, series of studies

My hands were *coarse* from all the washing.
Soup is served before the main *course*.
Only you can decide on the proper *course* of study.

coma (n)	prolonged unconsciousness
comma (n)	mark of punctuation

The woman was in a *coma* following the accident.
It is important to understand the uses of the *comma*.

command (n)	an order, direction, authority
(v)	to order, direct
commend (v)	to praise, to entrust

The director took full *command* of the situation.
His presence *commanded* attention.
I must *commend* you on an outstanding performance.

commence (v)	to begin
comments (n)	remarks
(v)	to make remarks

The meeting will *commence* after lunch.
His *comments* were not called for.
She *comments* after everything I say.

complement (n)	that which completes
(v)	to complete, go well with
compliment (n)	expression of praise
(v)	to express praise

A full *complement* of soldiers arrived.
That color will *complement* your room.
Your *compliment* was most appreciated.
I will *compliment* the student on her outstanding work.

| confidant (n) | trusted friend or adviser (*confidante* for female) |
| confident (n) | sure, certain |

Eric's *confidante* is Carole Sheridan.
I am *confident* that you will be successful.

| conscience (n) | the sense of right and wrong |
| conscious (adj) | aware, having feeling |

After the confession, his *conscience* was clear.
Are you *conscious* of your actions?

continual (adj)	occurring steadily or recurring frequently
continuous (adj)	happening without interruption

The bells ring every hour on a *continual* basis.
The *continuous* noise made him very nervous.

cooperation (n)	joint effort
corporation (n)	a form of business organization

Your *cooperation* will be greatly appreciated.
The *corporation* is moving its headquarters to Main Street.

correspondence (n)	letters
correspondents (n)	those who write

Your *correspondence* reached me this morning.
The *correspondents* had a brief meeting yesterday.

costume (n)	style of clothing
custom (n)	usual practice or habit

Her *costume* was very appropriate.
It is a *custom* for people to greet each other properly.

council (n)	an assembly
counsel (n)	an attorney, advice
(v)	to advise
consul (n)	a foreign representative

The Town *Council* will have a brief meeting this evening.

The plaintiff's *counsel* made a moving plea.
The teacher will *counsel* any student who asks.
The *consul* was granted diplomatic immunity.

credible (adj)	believable, reliable
creditable (adj)	deserving of credit
credulous (adj)	too easily convinced

She is a *credible* witness.
The soldier's bravery was *creditable*.
The lying witness convinced the *credulous* jury.

currant (n)	small fruit, berry
current (adj)	belonging to the present

They purchased a jar of *currant* jelly.
Is this the *current* issue of the magazine?

decease (v)	to die
disease (n)	an illness

Mr. Murphy has been *deceased* since 1970.
Unfortunately, his *disease* was not curable.

decent (adj)	proper, reasonably good
descent (n)	a going down, decline
dissent (n)	disagreement

He seems to be a *decent* fellow.
The *descent* from the mountain was tiring.
The problem caused much *dissent* among the normally united group.

decree (n)	official order or decision
degree (n)	successive step, measured amount

The *decree* seemed to be reasonable.
There are different *degrees* of efficiency.

defer (v)	to put off
differ (v)	to disagree

We will *defer* your payment for only one month.
The two men *differ* in their opinions.

deference (n)	a yielding of opinion, regard for another's wishes
difference (n)	dissimilarity

In *deference* to the dignitary, I will not press the issue.
There seems to be a slight *difference* of opinion.

depraved	past participle of *deprave*, morally corrupted
deprived	past participle of *deprive*, underprivileged, forced to do without

The *depraved* witness ranted and raved.
You will not be *deprived* of any necessities.

deserts (n)	deserved award or punishment
desert (n)	barren region
(v)	forsake, leave
dessert (n)	last course of a meal

The scofflaw received his just *deserts* when his car was impounded.
The oasis in the *desert* was actually a mirage.
It is terrible to *desert* one's child.
For *dessert*, we ordered apple pie.

device (n)　　　　　plan, scheme, contrivance
devise (v)　　　　　to contrive, plan

> A new mechanical *device* will be necessary to start the machine.
>
> She *devised* a plan of action that should work.

disapprove (v)　　　to consider wrong
disprove (v)　　　　to prove the falsity of

> I *disapprove* of immoral actions.
>
> The attorney tried to *disprove* the statement of the witness.

disburse (v)　　　　to pay out, expend
disperse (v)　　　　to break up, scatter

> I *disbursed* $25 on your behalf.
>
> The mob *dispersed* when the police arrived.

do (v)　　　　　　　to perform
due (adj)　　　　　owing or scheduled to arrive
dew (n)　　　　　　moisture

> You cannot leave until you *do* your chores.
>
> My mortgage payment is *due* on the tenth of each month.
>
> The *dew* settled on the ground.

done　　　　　　　past participle of *do*, completed
dun (v)　　　　　　demand payment

> I have *done* all my chores.
>
> Pay your bills, and we will not have to *dun* you.

dose (n)	extent of treatment, measured quantity
doze (v)	to nap

Take a small *dose* of the medicine.
The man *dozed* off for a few hours.

dual (adj)	double
duel (n)	a formal fight, combat

The knife has a *dual* edge.
Hamilton was killed in a *duel*.

dying	present participle of *die*
dyeing	present participle of *dye*, to color

The poor man is *dying* of cancer.
I am *dyeing* my dress red.

elicit (v)	to draw out, extract
illicit (adj)	unlawful

The candidate was trying to *elicit* money for the campaign.
They were having an *illicit* love affair.

eligible (adj)	qualified, fit to be chosen
illegible (adj)	difficult to read

The winner will be *eligible* for the $1 million drawing.
If your handwriting is *illegible*, you should consider typing.

emerge (v)	to rise from
immerge (v)	to plunge into, immerse

He *emerged* a winner.
The technician *immerged* the x-ray in a chemical bath.

emigrate (v)	to leave or move away from
immigrate (v)	to move to

The refugees *emigrated* from Russia.
They *immigrated* to America.

eminent (adj)	well-known, distinguished
imminent (adj)	threatening, impending
emanate (v)	to issue from, be emitted

He is an *eminent* politician.
I do not feel that there is any *imminent* danger.
A foul odor *emanated* from the kitchen.

ensure (v)	to make certain
insure (v)	protect against loss
assure (v)	to give confidence

I want to *ensure* your safety.
You should *insure* the package for $50.
Let me *assure* you, you are in no danger.

envelop (v)	to wrap, surround, conceal
envelope (n)	a wrapper for a letter

The members fled when smoke *enveloped* the room.
Do not forget to put your return address on the *envelope*.

everyday (adj)	daily (used before a noun)
every day	each day

Brushing your teeth should be an *everyday* activity.
For *every day* that you are late, there will be a penalty.

everyone (n)   each one
every one   each one (when followed by *of*)

> *Everyone* will be ready at eight.
> *Every one* of them will be ready at eight.

expend (v)   to spend, use up
expand (v)   to increase in size

> They *expended* all their resources on buying a home.
> They *expanded* the home by adding a den.

expansive (adj)   widely extended
expensive (adj)   costly, high priced

> The *expansive* bridge joined the two cities.
> *Expensive* does not always mean better.

fair (n)   festival, market, carnival
    (adj)   according to the rules, light in color
fare (n)   money paid for transportation

> I won this stuffed animal at the *fair*.
> I appeal to your sense of *fair* play.
> *Fair* skin sunburns easily.
> The *fare* has gone up to 50 cents.

farther (adj)   more distant
further (adv)   to a greater degree

> The drive from the airport was *farther* than we had
>   expected.
> We can discuss the proposal *further* at a later date.

faze (v)   to disturb, embarrass
phase (n)   stage of development

The incident did not seem to *faze* her.
We are now in the second *phase* of the project.

feat (n)	remarkable accomplishment
feet (n)	plural of *foot*

That was quite a *feat*!
My *feet* hurt after the mile hike.

finale (n)	conclusion
finally (adv)	in conclusion
finely (adv)	in a fine manner, minutely

The grand *finale* was beautiful.
He *finally* remembered to call.
She *finely* and tactfully handled the situation.

fineness (n)	delicacy
finesse (n)	ability to handle delicate situations, tact

The *fineness* of the embroidery impressed everyone.
You handled the situation with great *finesse*.

fir (n)	evergreen tree
fur (n)	pelt of an animal

Fir trees are beautiful when they are snow covered.
She received an expensive *fur* coat for her birthday.

fiscal (adj)	financial, pertaining to public revenues
physical (adj)	pertaining to the body

The *fiscal* period begins in July.
It is wise to have a *physical* examination regularly.

flair (n)	natural aptitude
flare (n)	a light or signal

She has a *flair* for design.
The *flare* warned them of impending danger.

flew (v)	past tense of *fly*, soared through the air
flu (n)	short for *influenza*
flue (n)	part of a chimney

The airplane *flew* at a very high altitude.
He was very weak after recovering from the *flu*.
You must clean your *flue* if you want to avoid a chimney fire.

flour (n)	finely chopped grain
flower (n)	blossoming plant

She used five pounds of *flour* to bake the bread.
He sent her *flowers* as a sign of love.

for (prep)	in favor of, in place of
fore (n)	front part of something
four (adj)	numeral

I will go *for* you if you are unable to attend.
In order to present the facts, he brought the witness to the *fore*.
I tried at least *four* times.

formally (adv)	in a formal manner
formerly (adv)	at an earlier time

They all dressed *formally* for the dance.
I believe that we were *formerly* classmates.

| fort (n) | enclosed place of defense |
| forte (n) | strong point |

The *fort* afforded them adequate protection.
Mathematics is not my *forte*!

| forth (adv) | forward, out |
| fourth (n) | following third |

Go *forth* and make an attempt.
On his *fourth* attempt, he crossed the hurdle.

| forward (adv) | ahead, toward the front |
| foreword (n) | preface in a book |

"*Forward*, march," yelled the captain.
The *foreword* offered valuable information about the
    author.

grate (n)	part of a fireplace
(v)	to irritate
great (adj)	large quantity, wonderful

The *grate* was covered with ashes.
The noise *grates* on my nerves.
You did a *great* job.

| guessed (v) | past tense of *guess*, estimated |
| guest (n) | visitor |

You *guessed* correctly.
Our *guest* arrived later than we had expected.

| hall (n) | large room |
| haul (v) | to pull with force |

The *hall* was beautifully decorated for the party.
I am tired; I cannot *haul* any more wood.

handsome (adj)	good-looking
hansom (n)	two-wheeled covered carriage

Richard Moeller is a *handsome* young man.
The *hansom* cab ride through Central Park was romantic.

heal (v)	to cure
heel (n)	back of the foot

Unfortunately, doctors cannot *heal* all their patients.
She had difficulty getting her *heel* into the boot.

hear (v)	to perceive by ear
here (adv)	in this place

I did not *hear* you when you called.
They are all *here*; we can start.

heard (v)	past tense of *hear*, sensed sounds
herd (n)	a group of animals

I *heard* the thunder last night and was frightened.
The *herd* of cattle trampled the rancher's land.

higher (adj)	comparative degree of high
hire (v)	to engage or employ

I scored ten points *higher* this time.
My services are not for *hire*.

holey (adj)	full of holes
wholly (adv)	completely
holly (n)	a shrub

That *holey* blouse should be thrown out.
I am *wholly* satisfied with the results.
The *holly* tree needs water.

| human (n) | a person |
| humane (adj) | civilized, kindly |

Every *human* should be free to make choices.
That was the only *humane* thing that could be done.

ideal (adj)	perfect
idle (adj)	unemployed, not working
idol (n)	object of worship

Michael Kaminsky is the *ideal* candidate for the job.
Idle machines are not productive.
Elvis Presley had always been my *idol*.

| incite (v) | to stir to action |
| insight (n) | clear understanding |

The speaker *incited* a riot by his remarks.
Eric Laurence has remarkable *insight* for one so young.

| instance (n) | example, case, illustration |
| instants (n) | particular moments |

In this *instance*, I must agree.
Our lives are mere *instants* in time.

intestate (adj)	having made no will
interstate (adj)	between states
intrastate (adj)	within a state

The man died *intestate*.
Interstate travel between New York and New Jersey

was hampered by the weather.
The New York State Thruway is an *intrastate* highway.

its (pron)	belonging to it
it's (contraction)	it is

The company fired *its* president.
It's too late to go to a restaurant.

knew (v)	past tense of *know*, perceived
new (adj)	not old

The chairman *knew* of the incident.
The *new* building attracted many visitors.

know (v)	to understand, perceive
no (adj)	not any

I *know* of a good electrician.
There is *no* chance of getting the appointment.

lapse (v)	to become void
elapse (v)	to pass
relapse (v)	to slip back into a former condition

The policy will *lapse* if it is not paid by the tenth of
   the month.
If you let too much time *elapse*, we will not reinstate
   the policy.
He regained consciousness and then *relapsed* into a
   coma.

later (adv)	more recent, after a time
latter (adj)	second in a series of two

I will return the book *later*.
Of Tom and Marc, the *latter* should qualify.

lay (v)	to place an object down
lie (v)	to recline
(n)	an untruth

Please *lay* the package down at the front door.
I would like to *lie* down for a while.
He told a *lie*, and he was punished.

lead (n)	a heavy metal
(v)	to guide
led (v)	past tense of *lead*, guided

The *lead* pipe was too heavy to lift.
The majorette will *lead* the parade.
The majorette *led* the parade.

lean (v)	to bend or incline
(adj)	thin, not fat or fatty
lien (n)	claim against property as security for a debt

If you *lean* against the post, it might fall.
That is a juicy, *lean* piece of steak.
The judge ordered a *lien* against Mr. Smith's salary.

leased (v)	past tense of *lease*, rented or contracted
least (n)	smallest in size

They *leased* the property for one year.
That is the *least* important thing on my mind.

legislator (n)	member of a lawmaking body
legislature (n)	lawmaking body

Each *legislator* is entitled to one vote.
The *legislature* voted in favor of the bill.

lessen (v)	to make less, decrease
lesson (n)	something that is to be learned, instruction

That will certainly *lessen* your chances for the position.

Take a *lesson* from what happened.

levee (n)	bank along a river
levy (v)	to impose a tax

The *levee* was dry due to the drought.

The government may *levy* additional taxes to balance the budget.

liable (adj)	legally bound, responsible
libel (n)	false written statements

You are *liable* for your promise.

Mrs. Jones is being sued for *libel*.

lightening (v)	making lighter
lightning (n)	atmospheric electricity

By *lightening* her burden, we helped her cross the street.

Jonathan was awakened by the thunder and *lightning*.

local (adj)	confined to a certain place
locale (n)	a particular place, setting for a story

That is a *local* issue; do not interfere.

I believe the *locale* was Virginia.

loose (v)	to set free
lose (v)	to suffer a loss, mislay
loss (n)	something lost

They set the animals *loose*.
Leave early, in case you *lose* your way.
He could not be compensated for the severe *loss* of
    property.

| mail (n) | correspondence |
| male (n) | masculine person |

The *mail* piled up while I was on vacation.
Every eighteen-year-old *male* must register for the draft.

| manner (n) | a way of acting, procedure |
| manor (n) | estate |

In what *manner* do you wish to proceed?
The *manor* stood amid the graceful willow trees.

marital (adj)	pertaining to marriage
martial (adj)	pertaining to the military
marshal (n)	an official

Marv and Barbara are having *marital* problems.
Martial law has been declared.
A new *marshal* will be chosen in two months.

| maybe (adv) | perhaps |
| may be (v) | might be |

If we don't receive his letter, *maybe* we should call.
Mr. Karp *may be* out of town tomorrow.

meat (n)	flesh of animals
meet (n)	an assembly or race
(v)	to come together
mete (v)	to measure, distribute

I like my *meat* rare.

The track *meet* was canceled because of the weather.

We will *meet* tomorrow for lunch.

The judge had to *mete* out the sentence based on the decision of the jury.

medal (n)	badge of honor
meddle (v)	to interfere
metal (n)	kind of element or alloy
mettle (n)	high quality, courage, spirit

For his bravery, he received a *medal*.

Do not *meddle* in the lives of others.

Gold is a very expensive *metal*.

Fran proved her *mettle* by her courageous act.

miner (n)	one who works in a mine
minor (n)	person under legal age

The California gold rush brought many *miners* to the West.

A *minor* cannot be sold alcoholic beverages.

mist (n)	haze, light fog
missed (v)	past tense of *miss*, failed to do

The *mist* was so thick we could not see the Golden Gate Bridge.

We *missed* you at the meeting yesterday.

moral (n)	lesson relating to right and wrong
morale (n)	spirit or mental condition

Many a story has a *moral*.

Morale was very low after we heard the bad news.

morning (n)   time before noon
mourning (v)   expressing grief

> The *morning* air is so clean and fresh.
> The man is *mourning* the death of his wife.

motif (n)   theme
motive (n)   intention or inner drive

> The *motif* for the party will be the fifties.
> We cannot determine a *motive* in this case.

none (pron)   not one, not any
no one (pron)   nobody

> *None* of the packages were properly wrapped.
> *No one* in the group had any objections.

ophthalmologist (n)   a doctor who treats eyes
optician (n)   one who makes or sells eyeglasses
optometrist (n)   one who measures vision

> Very delicate eye surgery was performed by the
>   *ophthalmologist.*
> The *optician* recommended oval frames.
> The *optometrist* determined his vision to be 20/20.

one (adj)   numeral
won (v)   past tense of *win*, triumphed

> *One* more chance is all you will have.
> The Yankees have *won* the World Series more times
>   than any other team.

overdo (v)   to do in excess
overdue (adj)   past due or late

It is unwise to *overdo* exercises when you are not in good shape.

Your *overdue* account will result in late charges.

packed   past participle of *pack*, bundled, pressed together

pact (n)   an agreement

The vase was *packed* in paper to avoid breakage.

The *pact* we made is binding on both of us.

pain (n)   suffering or strong discomfort

pane (n)   window glass

The patient experienced a great deal of *pain* after the operation.

The window *pane* must be replaced before winter.

pair (n)   two similar things

pare (v)   to reduce or peel

pear (n)   a fruit

The *pair* of shoes you like is now on sale.

You must *pare* an orange before you eat it.

I took the juicy, green *pear* from the fruit bowl.

parameter (n)   assigned value, reference for determining values

perimeter (n)   outer boundary or area

Certain *parameters* have been set, and we must abide by them.

The *perimeter* is larger than we had originally estimated.

partition (n)   division
petition (n)   formal request

> The *partition* has afforded the two secretaries much
>   more privacy.
> A *petition* is being circulated among the students.

passed (v)   past tense of *pass*, moved along, trans-
                           ferred, lead
past (n)   history, time gone by

> I *passed* your house on the way home from work.
> I will not reveal anything about your *past*.

patience (n)   endurance, composure
patients (n)   persons receiving treatment

> My *patience* is wearing thin.
> Dr. Zisman has many *patients* in the waiting room.

peace (n)   state of calm, freedom from war
piece (n)   portion or fragment

> We all wish for *peace* throughout the world.
> A *piece* of the pie is missing.

peak (n)   top
peek (n)   glance

> The view from the *peak* of the mountain was breath-
>   taking.
> Do not *peek* around the corner.

peal (n)   ringing of a bell
peel (v)   to strip off

> The *peal* of the church bells echoed through the hills.
> Many people will *peel* an apple before eating it.

pedal (n)	foot-operated lever
peddle (v)	to sell
petal (n)	part of a flower

Do not step so hard on the gas *pedal*!

You are not allowed to *peddle* your wares on this corner.

Each rose *petal* glistened from the dew.

peer (n)	equal in rank
pier (n)	a wharf or dock

You will be judged by a jury of your *peers*.

We could not see the *pier* due to the heavy fog.

perfect (adj)	flawless
(v)	to bring to completion
prefect (n)	an official

She is a *perfect* example of brains and beauty.

The writer must *perfect* the story before publication.

The *prefect* doled out the necessary punishment.

persecute (v)	to oppress, harass, annoy
prosecute (v)	to institute legal proceedings against

Many people throughout the world are *persecuted*.

The criminal was *prosecuted* for embezzlement.

personal (adj)	private
personnel (n)	staff, workers

The quarrel was brought about by a *personal* matter.

All *personnel* will be required to attend the meeting.

perspective (n)	appearance, point of view
prospective (adj)	anticipated, apt

When things look bad, you must keep your *perspective*.
The Greens have a *prospective* buyer for their home.

peruse (v)	to study or read
pursue (v)	to chase, follow, overtake

Peruse the contract carefully before signing.
The police had to *pursue* the suspect for an hour.

physic (n)	laxative
physique (n)	bodily structure
psychic (adj)	pertaining to mind or spirit

A *physic* will help to cleanse your system.
Exercising will help a person's *physique*.
A man with *psychic* powers was called in to help find the missing child.

plain (n)	flat field
(adj)	clear, obvious
plane (n)	tool to make level

Many pioneers perished attempting to cross the *plains*.
The *plain* truth is sometimes difficult to accept.
The carpenter used a new *plane* to smooth the surface.

plaintiff (n)	party instituting a lawsuit
plaintive (adj)	mournful

The *plaintiff* will call her first witness.
The *plaintive* cry of the wolf sent chills down my spine.

pleas (n)	appeals, statements, allegations
please (v)	to be agreeable

The attorney will enter two guilty *pleas*.
You cannot *please* everyone!

pole (n)	long, slender piece of metal or wood
poll (n)	counting, voting place, registering of persons
(v)	to count, canvass

The telephone *pole* toppled from the weight of the ice.

The *polls* will open at nine.

The students were *polled* for their opinions.

precede (v)	to go before
proceed (v)	to advance
procedure (n)	method (note the single *e*)

"A" *precedes* "B" in the alphabet.

The directions state: "*Proceed* to the second traffic light."

Filing this form is standard *procedure* for requesting a loan.

preposition (n)	part of speech
proposition (n)	offer or appeal

"Of" is a *preposition.*

Your *proposition* is too good to refuse.

presence (n)	existence, attendance
presents (n)	gifts
(v)	introduces formally

Your *presence* is required at a minimum of ten meetings.

Buy your Christmas *presents* early, and avoid the rush.

The emcee formally *presents* all of the guest speakers.

principal (n)	sum of money, school official
(adj)	main, first in rank, leading
principle (n)	rule, value

The loan, including *principal* and interest, amounted to $321.

The company's *principal* headquarters will be on Main Street.

A candidate should be a person of *principle*.

profit (n)	monetary gain
prophet (n)	one who forecasts future events

All the partners should show a *profit* from the merger.

The *prophet* foretold the events.

propose (v)	offer, suggest
purpose (n)	intention

I would like to *propose* a toast.

The *purpose* of our visit should be obvious.

quiet (n)	stillness
quite (adv)	considerably, completely
quit (v)	to stop, abandon

The *quiet* of the country was a pleasant change from the noisy city.

I am *quite* certain that I am correct.

Do not *quit* your job until you have found another.

rain (n)	precipitation
rein (n)	harness
reign (n)	term of a ruler's power

The *rain* helped to fill the thirsty reservoirs.
Adam held the *reins* with all his might.
A *reign* of terror prevailed under his dictatorship.

raise (v)	to lift, elevate
rays (n)	beams
raze (v)	to demolish or destroy

Raise your glass, and toast the new year.
The *rays* of the sun shone brightly on the newly fallen snow.
Construction crews will *raze* many of the old buildings.

rap (v)	to knock
wrap (n)	outer grament
(v)	to enclose

Rap twice, and I will know it is you.
You may need a warmer *wrap* this chilly evening.
Wrap the package securely.

rapt (adj)	engrossed, absorbed
wrapped (v)	past tense of *wrap*

Sheryl was held in *rapt* silence by the movie.
The meat was *wrapped* in aluminum foil.

read (v)	to perform the act of reading
reed (n)	a plant, musical instrument
red (adj)	a color

If one *reads*, one can learn a lot.
The *reeds* swayed with the breeze.
If you mix *red* and yellow, you get orange.

| reality (n) | actuality |
| realty (n) | real estate |

The *reality* of the situation did not hit us until later.
The *realty* office will close for the holiday.

| recent (adj) | of the near past |
| resent (v) | to be indignant about |

I saw your article in a *recent* issue of the magazine.
I *resent* that accusation!

| reference (n) | that which refers to something |
| reverence (n) | deep respect |

You will find the information in *reference* books.
His *reverence* for money created problems between
    friends.

| residence (n) | dwelling, house |
| residents (n) | people who reside |

This enormous *residence* should sell for over $100,000.
The *residents* of this home will be away for two weeks.

| respectfully (adv) | in a respectful manner |
| respectively (adv) | in the order listed |

The letter was signed, "*Respectfully* yours."
I gave the pail and shovel to Jack and Sandy *respec-
    tively.*

right (adj)	correct
(n)	just privilege
rite (n)	formal ceremony
write (v)	to inscribe

All the answers were *right* for a grade of 100 percent.
You have the *right* to sue.
Last *rites* were administered to the accident victim.
Please *write*, and let me know the answer.

role (n)	part in a play, function
roll (n)	register or list, small bread

This *role* will give her the opportunity to sing and dance.
The *roll* shows that you were absent twice last semester.

root (n)	part of a plant
route (n)	an established course of travel

Roots must receive water for the plant to grow.
You will find the shortest *route* by checking the map.

rote (n)	routine, repetition
wrote (v)	past tense of *write*

Marc learned his spelling words by *rote*.
I *wrote* a letter to you yesterday.

sail (n)	canvas part of a boat
(v)	to travel by water by means of sails
sale (n)	the act of selling, a selling at reduced prices

We had to replace the *sail* because of a large hole.
I would love to *sail* to Bermuda.
The store is crowded when it is running a *sale*.

scene (n)	a setting, place where something occurs
seen	past participle of *see*, observed

You could not have picked a prettier *scene* for the painting.

I had *seen* the accident on my way home.

seam (n)	line of junction
seem (v)	to appear

The *seam* on her dress was opening.

Things are not always what they *seem* to be.

sell (v)	trade or transfer for a price
cell (n)	a small compartment

Do not *sell* the stock until the price increases.

The prisoner was confined to his *cell* as a punishment.

seller (n)	one who sells
cellar (n)	level below ground

The *seller* dictated all the terms of the agreement.

Our *cellar* flooded during the heavy rain storm.

sew (v)	to stitch
so (adv)	in such manner, thus
sow (v)	to scatter seed

Bunny must *sew* the dress if she is to wear it tomorrow.

I will stay home *so* that you will be able to attend.

If you *sow* seeds in the spring, you can harvest them in the fall.

simple (adj)	not difficult
simplistic (adj)	oversimplified

This problem is *simple*.

You are sheltering yourself by taking such a *simplistic* viewpoint.

soared (v)   past tense of *soar*, flew
sword (n)   weapon

The airplane *soared* to great heights.
The *sword* pierced his skin during the duel.

some (adj)   part of
sum (n)   amount, total

Some of you will have to stay behind.
You owe me a large *sum* of money.

son (n)   male child
sun (n)   source of light

Marc Alan is my first-born *son*.
The *sun* disappeared behind the clouds.

stair (n)   a step
stare (v)   to look at

The rug on that *stair* should be replaced.
It is uncomfortable to have someone *stare* at you.

stake (n)   a pointed stick, prize in a contest
steak (n)   slice of meat or fish

Mr. Lorenz has a large *stake* in the outcome of this
   project.
The *steak* sizzled on the greasy grill.

stationary (adj)   fixed, not moving
stationery (n)   writing paper

Old schoolhouses had *stationary* desks and chairs.
Please order buff *stationery* and matching envelopes.

statue (n)	a carved or molded figure
stature (n)	height of a person
statute (n)	law or regulation

The *Statue* of Liberty has welcomed many foreigners.
The accountant is a woman of sizeable *stature*.
What is the *statute* of limitations for armed robbery?

steal (v)	to take unlawfully
steel (n)	a form of iron

If you *steal*, you can be arrested.
The *steel* strike created heavy unemployment.

suit (n)	set of clothes
(v)	to please or make appropriate
suite (n)	set of rooms, matched pieces of furniture
sweet (adj)	having a sugary taste

A dark business *suit* will be appropriate for the interview.
That style *suits* him.
Please reserve a *suite* of rooms for the conference.
Sugar will make your coffee *sweet*.

taught (v)	past tense of *teach*, instructed
taut (adj)	tightly drawn, tense

The child will have to be *taught* a lesson.
The rope must be *taut* or the boat will drift.

team (n)	group that works together
teem (v)	to abound

We will need a *team* of experts to make that decision.
The ocean *teems* with beautiful plant and fish life.

tear (n)	water from the eyes
tier (n)	a row or layer

A single *tear* fell from the clown's eye.
Your seat is located in the top *tier* of the balcony.

tenant (n)	one who pays rent
tenet (n)	principle or belief

The *tenant* pays the landlord $450 per month.
The basic *tenet* of his argument was implausible.

than (conj)	comparison expressing exception
then (adv)	at that time, next

Gold is more expensive *than* silver.
I will go home and *then* call you.

their (pron)	belonging to them
there (adv)	in that place
they're (contrac- tion)	they are

The students will receive *their* grades tomorrow.
Please place the packages over *there*.
They're making a very worthwhile investment.

therefor (adv)	for this, for it
therefore (adv)	consequently, as a result

I paid $1,000 for the car but received $1,500 *therefor*.
You will, *therefore*, have to surrender the merchandise.

threw (v)	past tense of *throw*
through (prep)	from one end to another, by means of
thorough (adj)	carried through to completion

Reggie Jackson *threw* the ball, and the runner was out.

If you look *through* the eyehole of a kaleidoscope, you will see a beautiful pattern.

They made a *thorough* investigation of the evidence.

to (prep)	toward, in the direction of
too (adv)	also, more than enough, excessive
two (adj)	numeral

We walked *to* the park.
He ate *too* much for dinner.
Eric has *two* rabbits, Bunny and Cinnamon.

trial (n)	examination, hardship
trail (n)	path

The defendant's *trial* is scheduled for March 20.
The rabbit left a *trail* in the newly fallen snow.

trustee (n)	one to whom something is entrusted
trusty (adj)	dependable

Raye appointed her nephew as *trustee* for her estate.
Her nephew is a *trusty*, hard-working young man.

undo (v)	to open, render ineffective
undue (adj)	improper, excessive

The man could not *undo* the harm that he had caused.
The attorney placed the witness under *undue* pressure.

urban (adj)	pertaining to the city
urbane (adj)	polished, suave

Urban living has many advantages.
The *urbane* gentleman charmed women with his wit.

vain (adj)	proud, conceited
vane (n)	device for measuring wind, weather-cock
vein (n)	blood vessel, bed of mineral materials

The woman went on a diet because she was *vain* about her appearance.

The weather *vane* spun furiously in the high wind.

His doctor thought the *vein* might be blocked by a blood clot.

| vendee (n) | purchaser |
| vendor (n) | seller |

The *vendee* paid $1 million for the purchase of the property.

The *vendor* received $1 million for the sale of the property.

vice- (adj)	prefix for designated titles of office
vice (n)	moral failing
vise (n)	a clamp

She was appointed *vice-president* in charge of sales.

Smoking and alcohol are two of his many *vices*.

The *vise* held the wood in place.

waist (n)	middle part of the body
waste (n)	needless destruction or expenditure
(v)	to expend needlessly

The belt fit snugly around her *waist*.

The *waste* of time was completely unnecessary.

If you *waste* money, you will have none left when needed.

| wait (v) | to stay, remain |
| weight (n) | heaviness |

I have to *wait* for my friend.
His excessive *weight* made it difficult to buy clothes.

| waive (v) | to forego, relinquish |
| wave (n) | gesture, surge of water |

The bank will *waive* all penalties.
The crested *wave* broke against the sandy, white beach.

wares (n)	goods for sale
wear (v)	to have on, carry on your person
were (v)	form of *to be*
where (adv)	in, at, at the place

The vendor sold his *wares* on the busy corner.
The bride will *wear* a satin gown to her wedding.
Where were you last night?

| way (n) | direction, distance, manner |
| weigh (v) | to find the weight of |

Which *way* to San Francisco?
It is best to *weigh* yourself in the morning.

| weak (adj) | lacking strength |
| week (n) | period of seven days |

You are too *weak* to lift the piece of furniture.
We will meet for lunch on Wednesday of next *week*.

weather (n)	condition of the atmosphere
(v)	to come through safely
whether (conj)	if, in case

We cannot do much about the *weather*.
If properly dressed, you will *weather* the storm.
Find out *whether* this contract is acceptable.

who's (contraction)	who is, who has
whose (pron)	possessive of *who*, belonging to whom

"*Who's* there?" the woman called.
Please tell me *whose* paper this is.

woman (n)	female person
women (n)	female people

The *woman* left her coat at the restaurant.
The *women* left their coats at the restaurant.

your (pron)	belonging to you
you're (contraction)	you are

Please make sure to gather *your* belongings before leaving.
You're a very lucky person.

CHAPTER 9

ABBREVIATIONS

Academic Degrees, Acronyms, Broadcasting Systems, Companies and Organizations, Compass Points, Geographical Terms, Government Agencies, Measurements, Titles, Commonly Used Abbreviations

The abbreviation serves as a space-saving device and is widely used in tables, footnotes, invoices, and so forth. Careful writers, however, avoid using abbreviations in the body of most written material. The rule of thumb among writers is, "If in doubt, write it out."

When using abbreviations, you must be certain that the intended reader will understand your reference. When you hear or see *CIA*, for example, you undoubtedly think of the Central Intelligence Agency. Are you aware that the Culinary Institute of America bears the same initials? Confusion can be avoided by writing out your intended reference followed by the abbreviation in parentheses.

A recent report published by the American Bar Association (ABA). . . . The ABA further reports . . .

Leading authorities cannot agree on the capitalization or punctuation of many abbreviations; therefore, it is wise to check a dictionary and to be consistent within the same written material.

Abbreviations that have no periods are typed with no space between the letters; abbreviations that have periods are typed with no spaces after the inside periods and one at the conclusion of the abbreviation. (The exception to this latter rule is personal names: H. G. Wells.)

The following guidelines should be of value.

Academic Degrees

Academic degrees that appear at the end of a name are abbreviated, using capital letters with a period after each part.

> Susan Bergstein, R.N.
> Marvin Karp, Ph.D.
> Janice Teisch, M.A.

Acronyms

An acronym is a word that derives from its initial letters. *NATO* (North American Treaty Organization) is an acronym whereas *FBI* (Federal Bureau of Investigation) is not. In the latter, you say each letter and do not use the initials as a word. Most acronyms are commonly used abbreviations and are easily recognizable. Each letter is placed in capital letters and periods are avoided.

> CORE (Congress of Racial Equality)
> NOW (National Organization of Women)

OPEC (Organization of Petroleum-Exporting Countries)
ZIP (Zone Improvement Plan)

Broadcasting Systems

All television and radio stations are written in capital letters
with no periods.

ABC (American Broadcasting Company)
CBS (Columbia Broadcasting System)
Station WQXR-FM

Companies and Organizations

When uncertain whether a company writes out or abbre-
viates parts of its name, check the letterhead or a telephone
book, if available. *Inc.* and *Ltd.* are commonly abbreviated;
the ampersand (&) can be either the symbol or word *and.* If
in doubt, write it out.

Many well-known business firms, unions, agencies, and so
forth commonly abbreviate their names. These abbreviations
are usually written without periods.

AT&T (American Telephone & Telegraph Com-
   pany)
FCC (Federal Communications Commission)
IBM (International Business Machines)
YMCA (Young Men's Christian Association)

Compass Points

Compass points are generally written out unless they follow a street address or designate a section of a city.

> 356 Washington Avenue, N.E.
> 124 East Fifth Avenue

Geographical Terms

Names of countries, cities, and states should usually be written out. Exceptions include:

1. U.S.A., U.S.S.R., U.A.R. (periods inserted)
2. Two-letter state abbreviations on envelopes and inside addresses. (no periods used) A list of such abbreviations can be found in the "Postal Services" chapter.
3. St. Louis, but Fort Lauderdale. If in doubt about others, check a dictionary.

Government Agencies

Well-known agencies (national and international) are often abbreviated with all capital letters and no periods.

> FDA (Food and Drug Administration)
> HEW (Department of Health, Education, and Welfare)
> IRS (Internal Revenue Service)
> UN (United Nations)

Measurements

Units of measure (weights, distances, etc.) should not be abbreviated except in technical writings, tables, and some business forms, with the exception of temperature measures.

The 50-gallon container rolled off the truck.
The weatherman reported a delightful 75°F for tomorrow.

Titles

Personal titles that appear before and after names are generally abbreviated. You capitalize the first letter and place a period after the final letter.

Mrs. Elaine Nicolucci
Hon. Ethel Lorenz
Carl Wanderman, Esq. (attorney)
Dr. Howard Rosen

Commonly Used Abbreviations

AA	Alcoholics Anonymous, American Airlines
A.A.	Associate of Arts (degree)
AAA	American Automobile Association
A.A.S.	Associate in Applied Science (degree)
ABA	American Bar Association, American Bankers Association
abbr.	abbreviation

ABC	American Bowling Congress, American Broadcasting Company
a/c or acct.	account
ACLU	American Civil Liberties Union
A.D.	(*anno Domini*) after the death of Christ
addl.	additional
ad val. or A/V	(*ad valorum*) according to value
AFL-CIO	American Federation of Labor and Congress of Industrial Organizations
a.k.a. or a/k/a	also known as
a.m. (AM)	(*ante meridiem*) before noon
AMA	American Medical Association American Management Association
AMEX	American Stock Exchange
amt.	amount
anon.	anonymous
a/o	(on) account of
app.	appendix
ARMA	Association of Record Managers and Administrators
ASAP	as soon as possible
ASPCA	American Society for the Prevention of Cruelty to Animals
ASTA	American Society of Travel Agents, Inc.
att.	attached
atty.	attorney
A/V	audiovisual
Ave.	Avenue
avg.	average
AWOL	absent without leave (military term)
B.A.	Bachelor of Arts (degree)
bal.	balance

BASIC	Beginners' All-Purpose Symbolic Instruction Code (computer language)
B.B.A.	Bachelor of Business Administration (degree)
BBB	Better Business Bureau
BBC	British Broadcasting Corporation
bbl.	barrel
B.C.	before Christ
B/L	bill of lading
bldg.	building
Blvd.	Boulevard
Bro.	Brother
Bros.	Brothers
B/S	bill of sale
B.S.	Bachelor of Science (degree)
Btu	British thermal unit
bu.	bushel(s)
bx	box
C	Centigrade, hundred, or Congress
c. or ca.	(*circa*) approximately
CAB	Civil Aeronautics Board
CARE	Cooperative for American Relief to Everywhere
CB	Citizens' Band (radio)
CBS	Columbia Broadcasting System
cc	carbon copy (copies), cubic centimeter(s)
CD	Certificate of Deposit
CETA	Comprehensive Education and Training Act
cg.	centigram(s)
ch.	chapter
chg.	charge

c.i.f. or CIF	cost, insurance, and freight
cm	centimeter
Co.	Company
c/o	in care of
COBOL	Common Business Oriented Language (computer language)
c.o.d. or COD	cash (or collect) on delivery
cont.	continued
co-op	cooperative
CORE	Congress of Racial Equality
Corp.	Corporation
CPA	Certified Public Accountant
CPO	Chief Petty Officer (military term)
CPS	Certified Professional Secretary
cr.	credit
CRT	cathode-ray tube
CST or C.S.T.	Central Standard Time
ctn.	carton
cu.	cubic
cu. cm.	cubic centimeter(s)
cu. ft.	cubic feet
DA	District Attorney
D.A.	Doctor of Arts (degree)
D&C	dilatation and curettage (surgical procedure)
DAT	Differential Aptitude Test
d/b/a or d.b.a.	doing business as
D.B.A.	Doctor of Business Administration (degree)
D.D.	Doctor of Divinity (member of clergy)
D.D.S.	Doctor of Dentistry
dept.	department
dft.	draft

dis.	discount
distr.	distributor
div.	dividend, division
DJ	disc jockey
DJIA	Dow Jones Industrial Average
dls/shr	dollars per share
DMZ	demilitarized zone
DOA	dead on arrival
doz.	dozen
DP	data processing
Dr.	doctor
dr.	debit, debtor, drawer
D.S.C.	Distinguished Service Cross
D.S.M.	Distinguished Service Medal
DST or D.S.T.	Daylight Savings Time
dstn.	destination
dtd.	dated
DX	diagnosis
D/y	delivery
E	East
ea.	each
EA	Eastern Airlines
ed.	education, editor, edition
Ed.D.	Doctor of Education (degree)
Ed.M.	Master of Education (degree)
EDT or E.D.T.	Eastern Daylight Time
EEG	electroencephalogram
e.g.	(*exempli gratia*) for example
EKG	electrocardiogram
enc.	enclosure
end.	endorse, endorsement
EOM or e.o.m.	end of month
EP	European Plan
EPA	Environmental Protection Agency

ERIC	Educational Resources Information Center
ESP	extrasensory perception
EST or E.S.T.	Eastern Standard Time
ETA	estimated time of arrival
et al.	(*et alii*) and others
etc.	(*et cetera*) and so forth
ETD	estimated time of departure
et seq.	(*et sequens*) and the following
F or F.	Fahrenheit
fac. or FAX	facsimile
FDA	Food and Drug Administration
FDIC	Federal Deposit Insurance Corporation
Fed.	Federal
FHA	Federal Housing Administration
FIFO	first in, first out
fig.	figure
fl. oz.	fluid ounce(s)
FM	frequency modulation
fn.	footnote
f.o.b. or FOB	free on board
FORTRAN	Formula Translation (computer language)
frt.	freight
ft.	foot, feet
FTC	Federal Trade Commission
fwd.	forward
F.X. or FX	foreign exchange
F.Y.I.	for your information
g or gr.	gram(s)
gal.	gallon(s)
GAO	General Accounting Office
GM	General Motors

GNP	Gross National Product
GOP	Grand Old Party (Republicans)
GRE	Graduate Record Examination
gro.	gross
hdlg.	handling
hdqrs. or hq.	headquarters
HEW	Department of Health, Education, and Welfare
Hon.	Honorable
h.p.	horsepower
hr.	hour(s)
H.R. or HR	House of Representatives
HUD	Department of Housing and Urban Development
ibid.	(*ibidem*) the same
IBM	International Business Machines
ICBM	intercontinental ballistic missile
ICU	intensive care unit
id.	(*idem*) the same
i.e.	(*id est*) that is
ill.	illustration
in.	inch(es)
Inc.	Incorporated
ins.	insurance
int.	interest
inv.	invoice
I/O	Input/Output
IOU	I owe you
IQ	intelligence quotient
IRA	Individual Retirement Account
IRS	Internal Revenue Service
ital.	italics
ITT	International Telephone and Telegraph Company

IUD	intrauterine device
IWPA	International Word Processing Association
J.D.	Doctor of Jurisprudence (degree)
J.M.	Master of Jurisprudence (degree)
JP	Justice of the Peace
Jr.	Junior
J.S.D.	Doctor of the Science of Laws (degree)
JV	junior varsity
k.	knot
kg.	kilogram
kilo.	kilometer, kilogram
KKK	Ku Klux Klan
km	kilometer(s)
KO	knockout
kt.	carat
kw.	kilowatt
L	liter(s)
LASER or laser	Light amplification by stimulated emission of radiation
lat.	latitude
l., ll.	line, lines
lb.	pound(s)
lc	lower case
LIFO	last in, first out
LL.B.	Bachelor of Laws (degree)
loc. cit.	(*loco citato*) in the place cited
LPN	Licensed Practical Nurse
L.S. or LS	(*locus sigilli*) place of seal for signatures
LSD	lysergic acid diethylamide
Ltd.	limited
m.	meter, married, masculine

M	thousand
M.A.	Master of Arts (degree)
max.	maximum
M.B.A.	Master of Business Administration (degree)
MC	Master of Ceremonies, Member of Congress
M.D.	Doctor of Medicine (degree)
M.Div.	Master of Divinity (degree)
mdse.	merchandise
mfg.	manufacturing
mfr.	manufacturer
mg.	milligram(s)
mgr.	manager
mi.	mile(s)
min.	minute(s)
misc.	miscellaneous
Mlle.	Mademoiselle
mm.	millimeter(s)
Mme.	Madam
Mmes.	Mesdames, plural of Mrs.
mo.	month(s)
MO	money order
mph or m.p.h.	miles per hour
ms.	manuscript
MST or M.S.T.	Mountain Standard Time
Msgr.	Monsignor
mtge.	mortgage
N	North, net
n/30	net in 30 days
NA or N/A	not applicable
NAACP	National Association for the Advancement of Colored People
NAM	National Association of Manufacturers

NANA	North American Newspaper Alliance, Inc.
NASA	National Aeronautics and Space Administration
natl.	national
NATO	North Atlantic Treaty Organization
N.B.	(*nota bene*) note well
NBC	National Broadcasting Company
n/c	no charge, no credit
NCCJ	National Conference of Christians and Jews
No.	number
NOW	National Organization of Women
NRA	National Rifle Association
NSA	National Secretaries Association
nt. wt.	net weight
NYSE	New York Stock Exchange
OCR	optical character recognition
op. cit.	(*opere citato*) in the work cited
OPEC	Organization of Petroleum-Exporting Countries
OR	operating room
OSHA	Occupational Safety and Health Administration
oz.	ounce
p., pp.	page, pages
PBS	Public Broadcasting Service
pd.	paid
PDT or P.D.T	Pacific Daylight Time
PERT	Program Evaluation and Review Technique
pfd.	preferred
PGA	Professional Golfers Association
Ph.D.	Doctor of Philosophy (degree)
pkg.	package

p.m. or PM	(*post meridiem*) afternoon
P/N	promissory note
PO or P.O.	post office, purchase order
ppd.	postage paid in advance
PR	public relations
pro tem.	(*pro tempore*) for the time being
PS or P.S.	post script
PSAT	Preliminary Scholastic Aptitude Test
PST or P.S.T.	Pacific Standard Time
pt.	pint
PTA	Parent-Teacher Association
Q	question, query
qt.	quart
qtr.	quarter
qty.	quantity
RADAR or radar	radio detection and ranging
R&R	rest and recreation
R&D	research and development
RC	Roman Catholic
RCA	Radio Corporation of America
re. or ref.	reference
recd.	recorded
reg.	registered
req.	requisition
RFD	rural free delivery
rm.	ream(s), room
R.N.	registered nurse
ROTC	Reserve Officers' Training Corps
rpm	revolutions per minute
RR	railroad
RSVP	(*répondez s'il vous plaît*) please reply
rte.	route
S	South

/S/ or S/	signed
SALT	Strategic Arms Limitation Talks
SAT	Scholastic Aptitude Test
sc., scil., or ss.	(*scilicet*) namely
SDS	Students for a Democratic Society
SE	southeast
SEATO	Southeast Asia Treaty Organization
sec.	secretary, section, second
SEC	Securities and Exchange Commission
SOS	call for help
sq. ft.	square foot
sq. in.	square inch
Sr.	Senior
SRO	standing room only
SSS	Selective Service System
St.	street
stats	statistics
stet	let it stand (proofreading)
syn.	synonymous
TB	tuberculosis
t.b.	trial balance
TBA	to be announced
TELEX or Telex	Teletypewriter Exchange
TGIF	Thank God It's Friday!
Th.D.	Doctor of Theology (degree)
TKO	technical knockout (boxing)
TLC	tender loving care
TNT	trinitrotoluene (dynamite)
treas.	treasurer
TV	television
TVA	Tennessee Valley Authority
TWA	Trans World Airlines, Inc.
TWX	Teletypewriter Exchange
UAR	United Arab Republic

UAW	United Automobile Workers
u.c.	upper case
UFO	unidentified flying object
UGT	urgent
UK	United Kingdom
UL	Underwriters' Laboratory
UN	United Nations
UNESCO	United Nations Educational, Scientific, and Cultural Organization
UPI	United Press International
UPS	United Parcel Service
U.S.A. or USA	United States of America, United States Army
USM	United States Mail
USMA	United States Military Academy
USN	United States Navy
USO	United Service Organizations
U.S.S.R. or USSR	Union of Soviet Socialist Republics
U/w	underwriter
VFW	Veterans of Foreign Wars
VIP	very important person
viz.	(*videlicit*) namely
vol.	volume
VP	vice-president
vs. or v.	versus
W	West
WATS	Wide-Area Telephone Service
whsle.	wholesale
wk.	week(s)
w/o	without
WP	word processing
wpm	words per minute
wt.	weight
yd.	yard(s)

YMCA	Young Men's Christian Association
YMHA	Young Men's Hebrew Association
yr.	year(s)
YWCA	Young Women's Christian Association
YWHA	Young Women's Hebrew Association
ZIP	Zone Improvement Plan
ZPG	zero population growth

Part II. Secretarial Techniques and Procedures

CHAPTER 10

LETTERS, MEMOS, AND POSTAL CARDS

Letter Styles, Standard Letter Parts, Two-Page Letters, Envelopes, Two-Letter State Abbreviations, Interoffice Memos, Postal Cards

We are a nation that creates paperwork—and letters and memos are the second most common type of business communication, after forms.

Whether your letter is dictated by your employer or originated by you, its organization, completeness, accuracy, clarity, and neatness are your responsibility. When your letter is typed, it should be one on which you are proud to place your signature or reference initials.

Letter Styles

Your letter should be vertically and horizontally centered so that the margins form an imaginary frame around the typewritten portion. The following guidelines should assist you in determining your horizontal and vertical spacing.

a short letter (approximately 125 words or less)
vertical spacing: 19–20 lines from the top
horizontal spacing: 17–67 margins (pica)
                    25–75 margins (elite)

an average letter (approximately 126–225 words)
vertical spacing: 15–18 lines from the top
horizontal spacing: 17–67 margins (pica)
                    20–80 margins (elite)

a long letter (approximately 226 words or more)
vertical spacing: 10–12 lines from the top
horizontal spacing: 12–72 margins (pica)
                    15–85 margins (elite)

Samples of some of the most common letter styles are shown on pages 179–182.

Standard Letter Parts

(1) DATE LINE

The current date, using no abbreviations, starts on vertical line 15–18 for a standard letter. For horizontal placement, see *Letter Styles*.

September 16, 1983

(2) MAILING OR IN-HOUSE NOTATIONS

Mailing notations (special delivery, certified mail, registered mail, air mail, by messenger) or in-house notations (personal, confidential) are placed two lines below the date either in all capital letters or underscored.

CONFIDENTIAL   or   <u>Confidential</u>

(3) INSIDE ADDRESS

The inside address starts four spaces below the date line (or two below the mailing or in-house notation, if applicable) and includes the name of the person to whom you are writing; the name of the company, if applicable; the street address; and the name of the city, state, and ZIP code.

Whether or not the title should appear on the same line as the name will be determined by the length. Try to square the inside address as much as possible.

The two-letter state abbreviation is used for the inside address. (See the end of this section for a complete listing.) The state name should be written out if appearing in the body of the letter.

> Mrs. Bunny Feiler, President
> X & Z Company, Incorporated
> 210 Park Avenue South
> New York, NY 10003

The inside address should always consist of at least three lines. When you have a company with no street address, such as would be located in a very small town, place the state and ZIP code under the city.

> ABC Company
> Small Town
> State, 00000

NOTE: Refer to the chapters entitled "Capitalization" and "Numbers" for further information regarding the inside address.

(4) ATTENTION LINE

The attention line is used when you are writing directly to the company and want the letter directed to a particular person and/or department. The salutation, therefore, is always *Gentlemen.*

> ATTENTION ELSIE HERSCH (capitals with no colon)
> Attention Personnel Manager
> Attention: Accounting Department

The attention line is placed on the envelope as follows:

P & M Construction Company 345 Madison Avenue Columbus, OH 43004 ↓ 2 *(double space)* Attention: Paul Sharfin ↓ 2	P & M Construction Company Attention: Paul Sharfin 345 Madison Avenue Columbus, OH 43004

(5) SALUTATION

The salutation is placed two lines below the address or attention line (whichever appears last) and should correspond directly to the first line of the inside address. With mixed punctuation, a colon follows the salutation. With open punctuation, no mark follows the salutation or the complimentary closing.

Mr. John Smith	Dear Mr. Smith: Dear John: (informal)
Mrs. Joan Smith	Dear Mrs. Smith: Dear Joan: (informal)

Ms. Jean Smith	Dear Ms. Smith:
	Dear Jean: (informal)
Mr. and Mrs. John Smith	Dear Mr. and Mrs. Smith:
	Dear John and Joan: (informal)
Messrs. Max and Harry Lorenz	Dear Messrs. Lorenz:
	Dear Max and Harry: (informal)
Mmes. Ethel and Marilyn Lorenz	Dear Mmes. Lorenz:
	Dear Ethel and Marilyn: (informal)
The Comptroller	Dear Sir: (male)
	Dear Madam: (female)
A & D Shoppes	Gentlemen:
	Ladies: (if corporation of women)

NOTE: Refer to chapter 16 "Forms of Address," for government officials, military personnel, religious officials and education officials.

(6) SUBJECT LINE

This is considered part of the letter, not the heading; therefore, it should always be placed two spaces below the salutation. The purpose of the subject line is to direct the reader to the theme of the letter. The subject line can be in all capital letters, or underscored, or neither. The horizontal placement will depend on the letter style.

> SUBJECT: ACCOUNT NO. 8198
> Subject: Policy No. 721135
> Re: Introductory Magazine Offer
> In re: Invoice No. 343635

(7) BODY OR MESSAGE

The body of the letter is generally single spaced with double spacing between paragraphs.

a. The opening paragraph is relatively short and introduces the letter.
b. The middle paragraph(s) support the opening and/or provide additional information.
c. The final paragraph is short and serves as a summation, request, suggestion, or look to the future.

(8) COMPLIMENTARY CLOSING

The complimentary closing appears two vertical lines below the last typewritten line, and only the first letter of the first word is capitalized.

With mixed punctuation, a comma follows the closing. With open punctuation, no mark follows.

formal: Yours truly, Very truly yours, Yours very truly, Respectfully, Respectfully yours,

informal: Sincerely, Sincerely yours, Cordially, Cordially yours,

personal: Best wishes, As always, Regards, Kindest regards,

NOTE: Refer to chapter 16, "Forms of Address," for government officials, military personnel, religious officials, and education officials.

(9) SIGNATURE LINE

Horizontal placement depends on the letter. Personal signatures can be handled in any of the following ways:

Very truly yours,

Christine Nicolucci

Secretary to Mr. Lorenz

Very truly yours,

Harry Lorenz

Harry Lorenz
Assistant Manager

Very truly yours,

Christine Nicolucci

Ms. Christine Nicolucci

Very truly yours,

(Ms.) *Christine Nicolucci*

Christine Nicolucci

Unless both the name and title are short, it is best to separate them on different lines, with no comma. Allow at least four vertical spaces between the complimentary closing and the typed name so that a person with a large handwriting will have room for his/her signature.

Some companies prefer to have their names appear in this portion of the letter.

Very truly yours,

↓2

A & G PIE COMPANY

↓4

V. Gasparre, President

Very truly yours,

↓2

A & G PIE COMPANY

↓4

V. Gasparre
President

The comma is used *only* when the title appears on the same line as the name.

(10) REFERENCE INITIALS

The initials are always typed at the left margin two lines below the writer's name and/or title. They include the writer's initials (first) and the typist's initials (second) or the typist's initials only.

HLorenz/jt	HL/JT
HL:jt	jt

Reference initials are omitted from personal letters and from letters that you are writing on behalf of your employer and signing yourself.

(11) ENCLOSURE NOTATION

The enclosure notation appears on the line directly below the reference initials when anything is being sent along with the letter.

Enclosure	1 Enc.
Enc.	Enclosure 2
Encls.	Enc. (2)
Enclosures	Enclosure:
	1. Purchase Order No. 123
1 Enclosure	2. Check No. 345

In some offices, when something is attached rather than enclosed, the word *Attachment* will appear in place of *Enclosure*.

(12) CARBON COPY NOTATION

When a copy of the letter is sent to a third person, a notation to that effect is made directly below the enclosure notation or reference initials.

CC: A. Karp	cc: A. Karp
CC A Karp	Copy to: A. Karp

In some offices where a photostatic copy will be sent instead of a carbon copy, the initials *PC* are used.

If the writer does not want to apprise the addressee that a third party will be receiving a copy of the letter, a blind carbon copy notation is made on the office copy and third party copy *only*. No notation is made on the original.

BCC: M. Cole	bcc M. Cole
BC: M. Cole	bc M. Cole

(13) POSTSCRIPT

A postscript should be used sparingly because it could be interpreted as an afterthought and indicate a lack of organization on the part of the writer. Sometimes, however, it is used for emphasis.

To include a postscript, merely double space after the last notation and begin your message. The *P.S.* notation is no longer used.

jt
Enclosure

I will call you for lunch next Monday!

The first of the sample letters that begin on the following page shows the standard letter parts just explained. The numbers in parentheses on the letter correspond to the part numbers given above.

LIGHTING & DECORATING, Inc.

RENTALS & INSTALLATIONS

Back Drops — Booths — Wiring for Hotel and Trade Shows

April 12, 19-- ———————————————— (1) Date Line

CERTIFIED MAIL ———————————————— (2) Mailing Notation

Marric Enterprises ———————————————— (3) Inside Address
Attention Thomas James ———————————————— (4) Attention Line
24 Blazer Way
Spring Valley, NY 10977

Gentlemen: ———————————————— (5) Salutation

Subject: Hunting and Fishing Contract ———————— (6) Subject Line

• SEARCHLIGHTS

• SOUND

• BALL FIELD
LIGHTING

• DISPLAY
LIGHTING

• FLOOD
LIGHTING

• FURNITURE
RENTAL

• N. J. STATE
LICENSE #3110

I am enclosing the contract we agreed upon stipulating
all the terms and conditions of the hunting and
fishing show that will take place at the Besen
Community College Field House during the week of
May 1.

Can we meet for lunch on either Monday, Tuesday,
or Wednesday of next week to finalize the details?
If neither of these dates is convenient, please call
my office so that we can arrange a mutually convenient time.

(7) Body
or Message

Sincerely yours, ———————————————— (8) Complimentary Closing

LIGHTING & DECORATING, INC.

Noel Christie, President ———————————————— (9) Signature Line

sll ———————————————— (10) Reference Line
Enclosure ———————————————— (11) Enclosure Notation
cc: Besen Community College ———————————————— (12) Carbon Copy Notation

The ski show contract will be ready next week.——— (13) Postscript

143 East Railway Avenue, Paterson, NJ 07503   (201) 345-1250

ATLAS FIVE AND TEN INC.

HILDE AND HELMUT FEILER

—

179 MAIN STREET
FORT LEE. N. J. 07024
(201) 947-2999

February 20, 19--

Mr. and Mrs. Benjamin Swartz
138 Tapia Drive
Paramus, NJ 07652

Dear Mr. and Mrs. Swartz:

Re: Account No. 94132

We are delighted to welcome you to our Atlas family of
charge customers. Your application for a charge account
has been approved, and our staff is waiting to make your
shopping a satisfying and pleasurable experience.

On the tenth of each month you will receive a statement of your
purchases, and you will have until the twenty-fifth of the
month to make your payment. From the outstanding credit
reputation you have earned, we are certain that your payments
will be made promptly, thus avoiding any service charges.

We are taking this opportunity to send you our latest catalog
so that you can take advantage of our easy shop-at-home
service.

Thank you for giving us the opportunity to show you why Atlas
has earned the fine reputation for high-quality merchandise
and superior service. Remember: "If we don't have it; you
don't need it."

Very truly yours,

ATLAS FIVE AND TEN INC.

Michael Feiler, President

sll
Enclosure

FULL BLOCK STYLE
This modern letter style is becoming more and more popular.
Everything begins at the left margin; nothing is indented.

OFFICE
ORegon 5-2043

Max H. Lorenz

PUBLIC ACCOUNTANT
408 WEST 14th STREET
NEW YORK, N. Y. 10014

ANSWERING SERVICE
BA 7-5816

November 14, 19--

Mr. Warren Bergstein
Business Club
103 Samuel Lane
Grasmere, NY 10305

Dear Mr. Bergstein:

Subject: New Tax Laws for 19--

It is with great pleasure that I accept your
invitation to speak to your membership about
"New Tax Laws for 19--" at your January meeting.

I would appreciate your having available an
overhead projector, a chalkboard, and a table in
front of the room where I can display literature
and current tax forms for distribution. Also,
please let me know approximately how many
members will be in attendance.

Immediately following my presentation, I will
gladly entertain any questions your members may
have, either of a general or personal nature.
I am certain that your members will find the
information both useful and informative.

Thank you for giving me the opportunity to address
your organization.

                              Sincerely yours,

                              Max H. Lorenz

ML/el

MODIFIED BLOCK STYLE

This traditional letter style is the most commonly used. Everything
begins at the left margin with the exception of the date line and
complimentary closing. Both start at the center or slightly to the
right of center.

April 15, 19--

Mr. and Mrs. Harry Lorenz
36 Lincoln Road
Monroe, NY 10950

Dear Mr. and Mrs. Lorenz:

Re: Scholarship Awards

On behalf of the faculty and staff at
Taylor Business Institute, I wish to congratulate
your daughters, Jacqueline and Nicole, for winning
one-half tuition scholarships for the accounting
program.

You can be extremely proud of their results
as there were many other competitors who took the
exam in your area.

Our early registration will be held on
Saturday, May 3 from 9 AM to 2 PM, and we look
forward to welcoming Jacqueline and Nicole to our
Taylor family.

Sincerely,

Marilyn Sarch, Dean

sll

291 Buehler Place at Route 17, Paramus, New Jersey 07652

SEMIBLOCK STYLE

This letter style is identical to the modified block style, except each paragraph is indented five to seven spaces from the left margin and the subject line is centered.

Real World Counseling Service
P.O. Box 502
Nanuet, New York 10954

(914) 352-3240
(914) 352-9113

April 21, 19--

Mr. Brian Karen
35 Amy Court
Highland Falls, NY 10928

RE: MARVIN BRIAN, FILE NO. 5857

I greatly value you as a client and would like
to be of service to you in the future should the
need arise.

Your son Marvin has successfully completed the
career counseling program designed especially for
him; and, as a result, is now gainfully and
happily employed. Yet, you have made no effort
to pay any part of the $250 which has been due and
owing since January.

As a business person, I know that you appreciate
those of your customers who meet their obligations
promptly.

Won't you, therefore, send me your check for the
full amount of $250 and retain the good credit
standing you have earned.

JANICE TEISCH, DIRECTOR

sll

SIMPLIFIED STYLE

This letter style is written in full block with the salutation and complimentary closing omitted. The subject line appears in all capital letters three lines below the inside address and three lines above the body. The writer's name appears four lines below the final paragraph, also in all capital letters.

This streamlined letter style has been recommended by the Administrative Management Society and is expected to be the trend of the future as it is less time consuming, thereby cutting costs.

Two-Page Letters

When typing a two-page letter, use letterhead for the first page and plain bond paper of the same color and weight for the second page.

When you divide a paragraph between pages, at least two lines must remain on the first page and two lines be carried to the following page. A three-line paragraph cannot be divided, and you *cannot* carry the complimentary closing to a second page without having at least two lines above it.

The heading on the second page should be as follows:

Ms. Jacqueline Kim   Page 2   October 12, 19—

or

Ms. Jacqueline Kim   –2–   October 12, 19—

or

Ms. Jacqueline Kim
Page 2   **Use this style for full block**
October 12, 19—

FOLDING THE LETTER

1. Standard (8½ by 11 inch) stationery being placed in a No. 10 (9½ by 4⅛ inch) envelope, Monarch (7¼ by 10½ inch) stationery being placed in a No. 7 (7½ by 3⅞ inch) envelope, or Baronial (5½ by 8½ inch) stationery being placed in a No. 6-¾ (6½ by 3⅝ inch) envelope folded as follows:

   a. Fold the bottom of the letter approximately one-third up and make a crease.
   b. Fold the top one-third down and make a crease.

2. Standard stationery being placed in a No. 6-¾ (6½ by 3⅝ inch) envelope is folded as follows:

   a. Fold in half, long side up.
   b. Fold in thirds across.

(a)

(b)

3. Stationery being placed in a window envelope will be folded as follows:

   a. Fold the bottom of the letter approximately one-third up and make a crease.
   b. Fold the top one-third back and make a crease. The inside address should be on the outside and placed in the envelope so that it is visible through the window.

(a)

(b)

Envelopes

ADDRESSING THE ENVELOPE

1. The address is single spaced in the block style. The address should appear on the envelope as it appears on the inside address.
2. All in-house notations (personal, attention, confidential, hold, please forward) should be typed two to three lines below the return address and should align with the left margin.
3. All postal notations (special delivery, certified mail, registered mail, air mail, by messenger) should be typed under where the stamp will be placed (approximately nine lines from the top.)

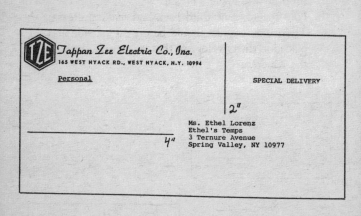

Tappan Zee Electric Co., Inc.
165 WEST NYACK RD., WEST NYACK, N.Y. 10994

Personal   SPECIAL DELIVERY

                    2"

                    Ms. Ethel Lorenz
                    Ethel's Temps
              4"   3 Ternure Avenue
                    Spring Valley, NY 10977

No. 10 envelope

4. Optical character readers (OCR) are now expediting the mail in many large cities, and the use of the OCR is becoming widespread. The Post Office is, therefore, suggesting that the following guidelines be followed for the increased accuracy and speed of mail delivery.

   a. The name and address should be typed in all capital letters with no punctuation. (Note the abbreviation of AVE, ST, BLVD, RD, etc.)

   > MR MORTON TEISCH
   > GRANTS UNLIMITED
   > 7 INLAND RD
   > SPRING VALLEY NY 10977

   b. If the addressee used both a street address and a post office box number, the line directly above the city, state and ZIP code is where the letter will be delivered.

   c. If a room or suite number is used, it should immediately follow the street address on the same line.

   > 56 FIFTH ST ROOM 304

   d. The five-digit ZIP code must be used. ZIP code directories can be purchased at any bookstore. When the nine-digit ZIP code is implemented, its use will be "entirely voluntary."

   e. The two-letter state abbreviation should be used on all mail.

   f. Names of cities, towns, and commonly used streets are also abbreviated.

   > Memorial Drive = MEM DR

Two-Letter State Abbreviations

Alabama	AL	Missouri	MO
Alaska	AK	Montana	MT
Arizona	AZ	Nebraska	NE
Arkansas	AR	Nevada	NV
California	CA	New Hampshire	NH
Canal Zone	CZ	New Jersey	NJ
Colorado	CO	New Mexico	NM
Connecticut	CT	New York	NY
Delaware	DE	North Carolina	NC
District of		North Dakota	ND
Columbia	DC	Ohio	OH
Florida	FL	Oklahoma	OK
Georgia	GA	Oregon	OR
Guam	GU	Pennsylvania	PA
Hawaii	HI	Puerto Rico	PR
Idaho	ID	Rhode Island	RI
Illinois	IL	South Carolina	SC
Indiana	IN	South Dakota	SD
Iowa	IA	Tennessee	TN
Kansas	KS	Texas	TX
Kentucky	KY	Utah	UT
Louisiana	LA	Vermont	VT
Maine	ME	Virginia	VA
Maryland	MD	Virgin Islands	VI
Massachusetts	MA	Washington	WA
Michigan	MI	West Virginia	WV
Minnesota	MN	Wisconsin	WI
Mississippi	MS	Wyoming	WY

When addressing foreign mail, enter the country name as the last line of the address block, two line spaces below the city line.

Interoffice Memos

The main purpose of the interoffice memo is to transmit ideas, decisions, and suggestions to another member or members of your organization. If an organization uses memos frequently, it will generally have the forms printed. The forms can be half sheets or full sheets, depending on the length of the message.

On a memo you:

Omit	**Retain**
inside address	body or message
salutation	reference initials
complimentary closing	enclosure notation
signature	carbon copy notation

1. Start the body of the memo three spaces below the heading.
2. Align the left margin with the typewritten portion of the heading, and set the right margin so that it is equal to the left.
3. Single space the paragraphs in block style, double spacing between each paragraph.
4. When typing a memo on a blank sheet of paper, start 1½ inches from the top. Any of the following headings may be used:

To: TO:
From: or   FROM: or
Date: DATE:
Subject: SUBJECT:

        Date: Date:
To: TO:
From: or   FROM:
Subject: SUBJECT:

5. Double space between each item in the heading, and proceed as for a printed memo form.

A sample memo appears on page 191.

Postal Cards

Because a postal card does not allow much room for a message, the inside address, complimentary closing, and written signature are often omitted from the side that carries the message.

Both sides of a sample postal card appear on page 192.

IBEW *International Brotherhood of Electrical Workers*

Local Union No. 363   •   Rockland and Orange Counties, New York

60 PHILLIPS HILL ROAD, NEW CITY, NEW YORK 10956   •   (914) 634-4801

TO: The Executive Board

FROM: Cosmo E. Damiani, Business Manager

DATE: September 16, 19--

SUBJECT: Insurance Plan

Please be advised that there will be a brief meeting on Thursday, September 22, at 2 PM, to discuss the following:

1.   Changes in Insurance, and

2.   New Employee Benefits.

All are expected to attend.

CED

sl

NOTE: Some executives choose either to sign or to initial the bottom of the memo.

Joan Sheridan
30 Besen Parkway
Suffern, NY 10901

2"

2" Ms. Sheryl N. Thomas
25 West Funston Avenue
Spring Valley, NY 10977

© USPS 1981

December 2, 19--

Dear Ms. Thomas:

Please be advised that the date of our
meeting is being changed to Friday,
December 9 at 2 PM.

If you are able to arrive a half hour
early, I will be able to brief you.

Joan Sheridan

CHAPTER 11

REPORTS, MINUTES, AND ITINERARIES

Reports, Styling, Tables and Charts, Footnotes, Bibliographies, Minutes, Itineraries

Reports

Reports represent the prime method an executive has for obtaining and communicating information. Reports are written in the third person and deal with facts, letting the reader form his or her own opinion.

A report can take the form of an outline, a memorandum, or a formal report.

OUTLINES

Some reports are written in outline form; some use the outline as a preliminary for a more formal report. The outline separates the data into divisions and subdivisions for easy identification.

In the sample outline on page 195, notice the use of capitalization for the divisions and subdivisions.

1. For the heading, use a standard style or a spread heading.
   a. For a *standard heading*, start at the center point (50

on an elite and 42 on a pica) and backspace once for every two letters and spaces. Then type the heading normally.

STANDARD HEADING

b. For a *spread heading*, start at the center point and backspace once for every letter and space. Then type heading leaving one space between letters and three spaces between words.

S P R E A D   H E A D I N G

2. The secondary headings (A, B, C) can be either single or double spaced, depending on the length of the outline. They always, however, start a double space below the major division.

3. Set the tab for each subdivision, which is indented four spaces.

MEMOS

For reports prepared in memo form, refer to the chapter "Letters, Memos and Postal Cards."

FORMAL REPORTS

1. Many executives require a draft of the report so that it can be revised and polished. A draft should be prepared with double or triple spacing so as to allow room for editing. Unless the draft is to be distributed to several people, it is unnecessary to make copies.

2. Prior to preparing the final report, a page-end indicator should be prepared. (This can be used over and over again.) The page-end indicator is placed behind the report page and helps control the vertical spacing. The numbers

SAMPLE OUTLINE

3

I.   FIRST MAJOR DIVISION

    A.   First Secondary Division

    B.   Second Secondary Division

    C.   Third Secondary Division

II.   SECOND MAJOR DIVISION

    A.   First Secondary Division

    B.   Second Secondary Division

    C.   Third Secondary Division

III.   THIRD MAJOR DIVISION

    4 A.   First Secondary Division
        1.   First third division
    4   2.   Second third division
        3.   Third third division
            a. First fourth division
    4   b. Second fourth division

    B.   Second Secondary Division
        1.   First third division
        2.   Second third division
            a. First fourth division
            b. Second fourth division

1–33 indicate the line on which you are presently typing. When you reach the middle of the page, lines 33–1 indicate the number of typing lines that remain on the page.

This is useful in determining not only when you are approaching the bottom of the page but also the precise placement of footnotes.

3. The formal report can contain any combination of the following:

title page	method
table of contents	conclusions
letter of transmittal	recommendations
purpose	synopsis
scope and/or limit	bibliography
hypothesis	appendix(es)

Styling

MARGINS

1. When a report is to be bound at the top, use one-inch side margins and a one-inch bottom margin. The first page should have a two-inch top margin, and all ensuing pages a one-inch top margin.
2. When a report is to be bound at the left, leave one and a half inches for the left margin. All other margins remain the same. For centering, the middle point becomes 54 on an elite and 46 in a pica.

PARAGRAPHS

1. Paragraphs should be indented five to seven spaces from the left margin.
2. The text in a formal report will generally be double spaced, with double spacing between paragraphs. When a text is single spaced, also double space between paragraphs.

PAGINATION

1. The first page of a report (or chapter of a report) is generally not numbered.
2. All subsequent pages should be numbered four lines from the top at the right margin for a left-bound report. For a

top-bound report, the number should be centered on the seventh line from the bottom. (Refer to page-end indicator.)

-2-

8
7
6
5
4
3
2
1

QUOTED MATERIAL

Long quoted passages are idented five spaces from the left and right margins and single spaced. The quotation marks are then omitted.

For other uses of the quotation mark, refer to the "Punctuation" chapter.

1"

PAGE–END INDICATOR

AN EXPERIMENTAL STUDY TO DETERMINE THE

EFFECT OF THE SPELLING TEST ON

THE ABILITY OF STUDENTS TO SPELL

Presented to

the Faculty of the

Department of Business Education

and Office Systems Administration

Montclair State College

by

Sheryl Lorenz

B.S., Saint Thomas Aquinas College

December 1981

TITLE PAGE

Although many styles are acceptable, the title page generally contains the name of the report; by whom it was prepared; the office, school, or institution from which it originated; the date on which it was presented; and, in many cases, to whom it was presented.

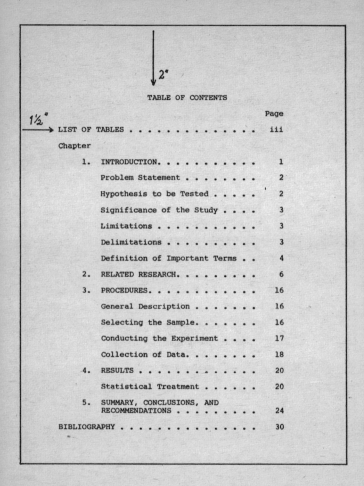

2″

TABLE OF CONTENTS

The table of contents lists subject headings and their respective pages.

2"

INTRODUCTION TO THE PROBLEM

Chapter 1

"Johnny can't read"; Johnny can't spell either. The

researcher and colleagues have a consensus of opinion that

1"

students graduating from our high school systems are deficient

in the area of spelling. This is evidenced by the lack of

spelling ability in transcriptions, in sentences, in basic

English drills, and in business subjects. At the postsecondary

level of a private business school, the students have one

year to hone their spelling skills prior to entering the

world of business.

Many of today's students were educated when basics were

forsaken, and the emphasis was on creativity. Educators,

viewing this alarming deficiency in the area of language arts

in general, are reaffirming the importance of a back-to-basics

education. It is, therefore, the responsibility of each

educator to seek ways to overcome this problem.

The researcher would like to determine whether the use

of weekly spelling tests will increase the spelling ability of

students in a private postsecondary business school.

This problem will determine whether it is worthwhile

for teachers to administer weekly spelling tests in order to

improve the spelling ability of students.

PAGE 1

The first page of your report is not numbered and starts on line 13
(two inches from the top). The margins will be one inch on the right
and one inch on the left. The report should end one inch from the
bottom of the page.

↓ 2"

BIBLIOGRAPHY

--> Helphill, Phyllis David. Business Communications With   <--
1"   Writing Improvement Exercises. Englewood Cliffs, NJ: 1"
        Prentice-Hall, 1958.

    Tuckman, Bruce W. Conducting Educational Research. 2d ed.
        New York: Harcourt Brace Jovanovich, 1978.

    Warriner, John and Sheila Y. Laws. English Grammar and Com-
        munication. New York: Harcourt Brace Jovanovich, 1973.

BIBLIOGRAPHY

This is a listing of all sources of reference and starts two inches from the top. The bibliography has one-inch side margins and five additional spaces are indented for added lines. The form is the reverse of a paragraph. (A detailed explanation of proper bibliographic style starts on page 211.)

Tables and Charts

UNRULED TABLE

WEATHER TABLE
↓2
Week of March 1
↓3

Day	Weather
↓2	↓2
Sunday	Sunny
Monday	Sunny
Tuesday	Rainy
Wednesday	Rainy
Thursday	Cloudy
Friday	Sunny
Saturday	Cloudy

RULED TABLE

WEATHER TABLE
↓2
Week of March 1
↓3

Day	Weather
↓2	↓2
Sunday	Sunny
Monday	Sunny
Tuesday	Rainy
Wednesday	Rainy
Thursday	Cloudy
Friday	Sunny
Saturday	Cloudy

TYPING EQUIVALENTS

> 6 lines = 1 vertical inch
> 66 lines = vertical lines on 8½ × 11 inch sheet of paper
> 10 spaces = 1 horizontal inch (pica)
> 12 spaces = 1 horizontal inch (elite)
> 102 spaces = horizontal sheet of paper (elite) (50 is center)
> 85 spaces = horizontal sheet of paper (pica) (42 is center).
> triple space (TS) = 2 blank lines
> double space (DS) = 1 blank line
> single space (SS) = no blank lines

TABLE DESIGN

1. Vertical placement

Determine vertical placement by counting all the vertical lines to be typed, including all blank lines within the typing area. Subtract the total number of lines to be typed from the total number on the page, 66.

$$
\begin{array}{r}
66 \\
- \underline{20} \text{ (lines to be typed)} \\
46 \div 2 = 23 \ (+1)
\end{array}
$$

Therefore, 23 lines must remain on the top of the table. Start typing on line 24 so that 23 lines are left blank.

2. Headings

The main heading is generally in solid capital letters and the subheading in initial caps. Double space between the main heading and subheading. Double space after the subheading in a ruled table and triple space after the subheading in an unruled table.

```
            HEADING
             ↓2
           Subheading
```

3. Horizontal Placement for Tables

a. Backspace-from-center Method

Clear all tabs and move margin stops to the end.

Determine the longest horizontal line in each column and decide on a standard number of spaces to use for the inter-columns.

From the center of the page, backspace once for every two character spaces in each column and once for every two spaces in the intercolumn(s), dropping any extra letter. Set the left margin at this point.

Space forward once for every character space of the longest line in the first column and once for each space in the inter-column(s). Set a tab at this point.

Repeat the same steps for each column.

b. Mathematical Method

Clear all tabs and move margin stops to the end.

Determine the longest horizontal line in each column and count the number of character spaces. Determine the number of spaces that will be used for the intercolumn(s). Add together.

Day		Weather
Sunday	10	Sunny
Wednesday		Rainy

Subtract from the number of horizontal spaces.

	Pica		*Elite*
	85		102
	− 26		− 26
	59		76

Divide by two so that half will be to the left of your column and half will be to the right of your column.

$$59 \div 2 = 30$$
$$76 \div 2 = 38$$

This is your left margin.

Space forward from the left margin as in the backspace-from-center method for tab stops.

4. Column Headings

Determine the longest line in the column and space forward once for every two character spaces. This will put you at the center of the longest line. Backspace once for every two character spaces in the column heading. Type the column heading at this point.

5. Horizontal Ruling

Determine the placement of columns, including a right margin.

To begin ruling, double space from the heading or subheading and make your first underscore. The second of the two lines in a double underscore is made by using the underscore key after moving your ratchet release (or line finder) slightly forward so that the second line will be close to the first.

After typing the last line of the column, double space from the original underscore to begin typing the table.

6. **Vertical Ruling**

Place a pen in the notch of the plastic cardholder at the desired place and press the index key. If your machine does not have an index key, turn the cylinder knob manually away from you in an upward motion.

cardholder
notch

Footnotes

Footnotes identify the source of a statement or direct quotation; identify the source of an unusual interpretation that has been reworded by you; or give credit for figures, illustrations, diagrams, definitions, or statistics. Footnotes are commonly typed at the foot of the page on which the reference number appears—hence the name. In some cases, however, footnotes are placed at the end of the report and are better termed endnotes.

TYPING NUMBERS FOR FOOTNOTES

1. Use arabic numbers.
2. Raise the reference number after the material to be noted

by turning the platen toward you. Leave no space before the number.

... it is final.[1] We will...

3. Leave two spaces after the footnote number.

PLACEMENT OF FOOTNOTES

1. Use the page-end indicator to determine the correct placement of footnotes appearing at the bottom of the page. As previously indicated, a report should end one inch from the bottom of the page. It is above this one-inch margin that the footnote will be placed. Inasmuch as the average footnote requires three lines, placement of one footnote will begin usually on line 11 of the page-end indicator.

```
                                                              11
                                                              10
     ‾‾‾‾‾‾‾‾‾‾‾‾‾‾‾‾                                          9
         [1]Kate L. Turabian, A Manual for Writers of Term    8
     Papers, Theses, and Dissertations (4th ed.; Chicago:     7
     The University of Chicago Press, 1973), p. 187.          6
                                                              5
                                                              4
                                                              3
                                                              2
                                                              1
```

2. For each additional footnote, start four spaces higher— three spaces for the footnote itself and one for the double space between. You must leave enough room to include a footnote for each reference number on the page.

3. Placement of the footnote remains the same, regardless of where on the page the text ends.
4. If the notes are placed on a separate page at the conclusion of the report, start 13 lines from the top of the page and center the heading, NOTES.

TYPING THE FOOTNOTES

1. Type an underscore from the left margin, approximately 20 spaces.
2. Double space below the underscore to start the first footnote.
3. Footnotes should be single spaced, with a double space between notes.
4. Indent the first line of each footnote five spaces.
5. Raise each footnote number slightly, and do not leave any space after the number.
6. Footnotes can be numbered in one of three ways: a) consecutively throughout the report; b) starting anew on each page; or c) starting anew for each chapter.

VARIATIONS

1. Some writers use an asterisk (*) in place of the footnote number when only one footnote appears in the report.
2. Some writers prefer to type the number on the line followed by a period and two spaces.

-----

1. Leonard Corwen, _Job Hunter's Handbook_ (New York: Arco Publishing, 1966), p. 14.

FOOTNOTE STYLING

Books with one author

[1]Claire Neff Eddings, *Secretary's Complete Model Letter Handbook* (Englewood Cliffs, NJ: Prentice-Hall, 1965), p. 56.

Books with multiple authors

[1]Carmella E. Mansfield and Margaret Hilton Bahniuk, *Writing Business Letters and Reports* (Indianapolis, IN: Bobbs-Merrill, 1981), p. 109.

Books with second or later editions

[1]Robert N. Corley and William J. Robert, *Fundamentals of Business Law*, 2nd ed. (Englewood Cliffs, NJ: Prentice-Hall, 1978), p. 503.

Books with no author's name

[1]*Webster's Legal Secretaries Handbook* (Springfield, MA: G. & C. Merriam Co., 1981), p. 387.

Books in a series

[1]Louis B. Wright, *The Cultural Life of the American Colonies, 1607–1763*, The New American Nation Series, ed. by Henry Steele Commager and Richard B. Morris (New York: Harper & Bros. 1957), p. 2.

Articles from a monthly magazine

[1]Sheryl Lindsell, "To Hire or Not to Hire...That is the Interview!" *The Secretary*, Jan. 1979, p. 8.

Articles from a weekly magazine

[1]Matt Clark and Mariana Gosnell, "Dealing with Dyslexia," *Newsweek*, 22 Mar. 1982, pp. 55–56.

Articles unsigned

[1]"New Ideas for Clean Elections," *U.S. News and World Report*, 4 June 1973, p. 79.

Articles from a daily newspaper

[1]Mariruth Campbell, "With the Artists—Lindsell at the Plaza," *Nyack Journal News*, 9 Feb. 1965, p. 7, cols. 1–2.

Bulletins, Pamphlets, or Monographs

[1]U.S. Department of Health and Human Services, Day

Care Division, *A Parent's Guide to Day Care* (Washington, DC: Government Printing Office, 1980), p. 1.

Unpublished Theses or Dissertations

[1]Sheryl Lorenz, "An Experimental Study to Determine the Effect of the Spelling Test on the Ability of Students to Spell," master's thesis, Montclair State College, Upper Montclair, NJ, 1981, p. 15.

Worked cited in the preceding footnote

[1]Ibid., p. 18. (Everything the same, except the page.)

[1]Ibid.,   (Everything the same.)

Bibliographies

Bibliographies, which appear at the end of a report, alphabetically list all the sources consulted, whether or not they have been footnoted.

PLACEMENT

1. The bibliography is typed on a separate page and starts on line 13, allowing for a two-inch top margin.
2. The word *Bibliography* is centered in all capital letters.
3. Both the left and right margins remain as in the report itself.

TYPING

1. Single space the entries, leaving a double space between entries.
2. Begin the first line of each entry at the margin and indent all subsequent lines five spaces.
3. Bibliographies contain the same information and basic style as footnotes, except for the following:

a. Entries are not numbered.

b. Specific page numbers are not referred to unless the work is part of a larger work with continuous pagination. In such cases, page numbers are included.

c. The author's name is listed in inverted order.

Karp, Arlene E.

d. Parentheses around the place of publication and publisher's name are omitted. A period precedes and ends this section except when it is followed by a comma and page numbers.

Gilson, Goodwin W. *Letter Perfect: The Accurate Secretary.* New York: Arco Publishing, 1977.

e. All entries are listed in alphabetic order. Some bibliographies separate books, periodicals, and unpublished sources under subheadings.

f. If a source is unsigned, it is listed by title. Disregard the words *The* and *A* when you are determining alphabetic order.

Minutes

The notes you take at a meeting must be accurate, but they do not have to be verbatim. If the meeting is to be very formal, your company might want a record of every word; they will probably allow a tape recorder to aid you, but you must obtain permission to use it.

If you are not accustomed to taking minutes, acquaint yourself with minutes of previous meetings so that you can apply the format. (See the sample on page 214.)

If you are expected to conduct a meeting, review parliamentary procedure as clearly explained in *Robert's Rules of Order Newly Revised*, the bible for conducting business meetings.

Keep in mind the following:

1. Record the date, time, and place of the meeting, and all those who were present. Also note the time the meeting commenced and adjourned.
2. Sit near the presiding officer so that you hear everything clearly and accurately.
3. Remain constantly alert so that each time a new topic is introduced, you are prepared to record the name of the person who introduced it, seconded it, and the main points covered.
4. Use your judgment; never expect any member of the meeting to tell you what is important. If in doubt, include it.
5. Record the name of each person who proposes any action, opinion, or plan.
6. Take verbatim notes on resolutions, amendments, decisions, and conclusions.
7. Have paper clips handy (attached to your notebook) so that you can tag any items on which action is to be taken after the meeting. This will aid you in picking out these duties before transcribing your notes.
8. Make certain that you have heard everything clearly. If unsure, ask for the unclear portion to be repeated. Names, amounts of money, and dates are of extreme importance.

Itineraries

When making travel arrangements (domestic or international), it is best to contact a travel agent. There is no out-of-pocket fee involved. The travel agent can plan an itinerary, making all the travel arrangements and supplying whatever

DIRECTOR'S MEETING

August 15, 19--

The regular monthly meeting of The Marric Corporation Board of Directors was held on Monday, August 15, 19--, at 9 AM, in the company boardroom. President Marc Allen presided.

The following members were present: Eric Laurence, Thomas James, Jeff Teisch, Steven Teisch, Martha Rones, and Ethel Lorenz.

The minutes of the July 14, 19--, meeting were read by the Secretary and approved.

President Allen suggested that a feasibility study to determine the need for a computer system be instituted. The matter was tabled, and President Allen requested that the members be prepared to vote on such a study at the September meeting.

Eric Laurence requested that the advertising budget be increased by 10 percent in order to reach this year's quota. The request was approved unanimously because the Advertising Department had cut expenses in certain areas.

Thomas James reported that sales on the new Model 30A fishing rods are better than expected. The line is expected to be expanded.

The next meeting will be held on Tuesday, September 15, 19--. The meeting was adjourned at 10:30 AM.

Respectfully submitted,
Ethel Lorenz, Secretary

information might be needed. The names of accredited travel agents are available from ASTA.

American Society of Travel Agents
360 Lexington Avenue
New York, NY 10017

Be prepared to supply the travel agent with the following information:
1. employer's name, company, business phone, and possibly home phone
2. cities to be visited
3. dates and times of arrivals and departures
4. transportation preference (mode and class)
5. lodging preference (many prefer certain hotels)

Next, it will be necessary to prepare an itinerary—a chronological, easy-to-read schedule of daily events. The itinerary should contain:
1. date, time, and place of departure
2. mode of transportation (confirmed)
3. date, time, and place of arrival
4. lodging accommodations (confirmed)
5. appointments and any information pertinent thereto
6. date, time, and place of departure
7. mode of transportation (confirmed)
8. date, time, and place of return

ITINERARY FOR ETHEL LORENZ

From May 1 to May 6

Monday
May 1

9:30 AM EST   Leave Newark Airport via TWA, Flight No. 205
                   (tickets in envelope)

10:30 PST   Arrive in Las Vegas – Reservations at MGM
                   Grand Hotel (confirmation attached)

7:00   Dinner with Andrea Teisch – phone her prior
                   to meeting at (702) 123-7654

Tuesday
May 2

9 AM   Convention at MGM Grand (program attached)

Evening   Free

Wednesday
May 3

10:30 AM   Leave Las Vegas Airport via Western Airlines
                   Flight No. 145 (tickets in envelope)

11:05 AM   Arrive San Francisco. Hotel reservations at
                   Sheraton Inn (confirmation attached)

Thursday
May 4

12 noon   Address San Francisco Bar Association in
                   Cypress Room of Hyatt-Regency (notes on 3 x 5
                   cards in briefcase)

Friday
May 5   No scheduled activities

Saturday
May 6

9 AM   Leave San Francisco Airport, Flight No. 56
                   (tickets in envelope)

5 PM EST   Arrive Newark Airport. Limousine will be
                   waiting.

                                       Enjoy your trip!

CHAPTER 12

POSTAL SERVICES

Domestic Mail, Special Services, International Mail, Hints for Reducing Postal Expenses

Postal rates are subject to change; therefore, this chapter will be limited to the services that are available, not the rates. (Current rates can be obtained from any local post office.)

Domestic Mail

Domestic mail encompasses mail sent within the United States and between the United States, its territories, and its possessions. It includes Army-Air Force (APO) and Navy (FPO [the *F* stands for *Fleet*]) post offices and any mail sent to the United Nations in New York City.

First-Class Mail includes sealed letters (typewritten, handwritten, carbon copy, or photocopy), postcards, business reply cards and letters, checks, and greeting cards that measure at least 3½ by 5 inches in diameter. Any piece of first-class mail will be returned unless sufficient postage is attached.

When a large manila envelope is being sent first class, this designation should be marked on the front and back of the envelope. Special envelopes with green diamond borders are intended for first-class mailing.

Second-Class Mail includes newspapers, magazines, and periodicals. Publishers and news agencies wishing to mail second class are required to obtain permits from the United States Postal Service and must adhere to all postal rules and regulations.

Third-Class Mail includes circulars, books, catalogs, seeds, cuttings, bulbs, roots, and plants weighing less than 16 ounces. Special rates apply to bulk mailing and to books, records, films, and various educational materials.

Fourth-Class Mail, also known as parcel post, should not be confused with the United Parcel Service. Parcel post includes material that does not fall into the first-, second-, or third-class categories and weighs 16 ounces or more. Rates are determined by the weight and distance the package is to be transported. Included in this category are catalogs, farm products, and miscellaneous printed matter.

Special Fourth-Class Rates include books that contain at least 24 pages and do not have advertising, 16mm (or narrower) films, educational material, printed music, loose-leaf pages and binders containing medical information, and printed test material.

Library Rates are available to libraries, schools, and nonprofit organizations.

Priority Mail includes first-class mail weighing 13 ounces or more. It is always sent by air with no guaranteed time of arrival.

Official Mail, with no postage affixed, can be sent by members of the United States Government. This includes franked mail (bearing a facsimile of the signature in the upper right corner) and penalty mail (bearing a penalty warning and "Official Business" notation).

Special Services

Special services must be transacted at the post office.

Registered Mail should be used when anything of monetary value is being sent (such as jewelry, negotiable instruments, and money); the rate charged is dependent on the amount of value declared. Registered mail must be sealed along all edges. Tape may not be used. At the time of mailing, a receipt is issued.

If the registered item is lost and a claim is properly filed, the sender can be compensated for the value declared (not to exceed $10,000), provided the sender has not and is not being reimbursed by a commercial or private insurance carrier.

Insured Mail can be insured for up to $200 and encompasses third- and fourth-class mail. If the package is lost or damaged, compensation will be made for the amount of the insurance.

Certified Mail is used when you are sending something of no monetary value; no insurance is available. The value of this type of mailing is that a return receipt can be requested, offering you proof the letter was received, to whom the letter was delivered, and the date of delivery. A slight fee is charged for each additional service.

Return Receipt for Registered, Insured and Certified Mail

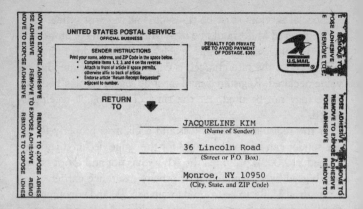

Gummed Side Pasted to the Back of the Envelope

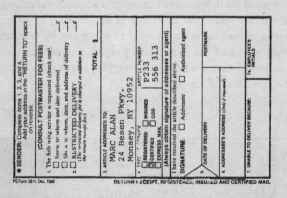

This Side Visible

Certificates of Mailing would be used when the sender requires evidence of mailing only. The fee for this service is substantially lower than that for certified mail.

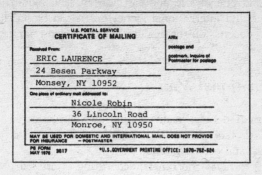

COD (Cash or Collect on Delivery) is used for first-, third-, and fourth-class mail where the addressee is responsible for payment of the postage and/or contents. The sender will receive a money order for the amount due.

Special Delivery provides the fastest delivery by messenger within certain limits of the delivery station during prescribed hours. It is available for all classes of mail.

Special Handling provides expeditious handling for third- and fourth-class mail, at a cost less than that of special delivery. This is necessary for parcels that are breakable or fragile and need special attention.

Express Mail offers a money-back guarantee that articles delivered to the post office by 5 PM will be delivered to the addressee by 3 PM the following day or can be picked up by the addressee by 10 AM the following day. Consult your local post office for additional options regarding urgent mail.

Mailgrams are transmitted via Western Union to a specific post office. The message is inserted in a window envelope and delivered by the receiving post office to the addressee.

Money Orders can be purchased and redeemed at any post

office and offer a safe and easy way to send money. Both domestic and international money orders can be purchased. The fee depends on the amount of money being transferred.

International Mail

International mail is divided into two categories:
1. LC (letters and cards), consisting of letters, letter packages, and postcards; and
2. AO (articles and others), consisting of printed matter, samples of merchandise, matter for the blind, and small packets.

When mail is directed to Mexico and Canada there is no additional charge. There are, however, higher rates and weight limits for overseas mail. Overseas packages must have a "customs declaration form" attached offering a description of the contents.

Hints for Reducing Postal Expenses

1. For certain types of mail, consider sending other than first class.
2. Keep your mailing lists up to date.
3. Presort your mail and take advantage of special presorted rates.
4. Use a postage scale, and have it checked regularly for accuracy so that you can be sure you are supplying your mail with the correct amount of postage.
5. Do not use special services unless they are necessary.
6. Obtain current postal charts.
7. Avoid using airmail for domestic mail because first-class mail is sent by air.

CHAPTER 13

TELEPHONE AND TELEGRAPH SERVICES

Telephone Services, Using the Telephone Effectively, Domestic Telegraph Services, International Telegraph Services

Telephone Services

DIALING INFORMATION

1. There is a slight charge for operator-assisted information calls within your calling area. Therefore, use the telephone directory provided by the telephone company. When it is necessary to contact the operator to obtain a local number, dial either 411 or 555–1212.

2. There is no charge for operator-assisted information calls outside your calling area. When such a number is needed, dial 1 + area code + 555–1212. (In some areas, the 1 is not necessary.)

3. Many organizations, in an effort to promote business, have adopted toll-free 800 numbers so that the caller will not have to pay to initiate the call. Before placing a long-

distance call, always check to see if an 800 number is available. Dial 1 + 800 + 555–1212. (Again, in some areas, the 1 is not necessary.) If you call toll-free numbers frequently, you should call or write for information about the directory available for a small charge from *The Toll-Free Digest Company*, Claverack, NY 12513.

TYPES OF SERVICES

Before placing a call outside your calling area, be certain that you have the correct area code. Also, when placing long-distance calls, be sure to calculate the difference in time zones.

Station-to-Station (direct distance dialing) calls save time and money. Place this type of call when you are willing to speak to anyone who answers. Merely dial the area code plus the number. This type of call bears the lowest rates, and charges start when the called party answers the phone.

Person-to-Person calls require operator assistance and are used when you are not certain that the called party will be available. Rates are higher than for the station-to-station calls, but there is no charge if the person you are calling is not available. Charges begin only when the called party (or extension) is connected. You dial 0 + area code + the number, and the operator comes on the line. Tell the operator that you are placing a person-to-person call and the name of the person to whom you wish to speak.

Collect calls also require operator assistance and are used when the person being called is expected to accept the charges. You dial 0 + area code + the number, and the operator comes on the line. Tell the operator you are placing a collect call. A collect call can be placed either to the number or to a particular person.

Wide-Area Telephone Service (WATS) is used by firms that make regular long-distance calls to designated areas. Ac-

Reproduced with permission of AT&T Co.

cess lines can be national, regional, or statewide; and rates are based on geographic area, not each call.

Mobile calls can be made to mobile units in cars, trucks, airplanes, buses, trains, and news services by contacting the mobile-service operator or by direct dialing.

Ship-to-Shore calls can be made to a person at sea by giving the long-distance operator the name of the ship, the person being called, and the number.

Conference calls can be accomplished with or without Dimension PBX equipment. You can contact the conference operator by dialing 0 and giving the operator the required numbers, names, and the time the call is to be put through. The charge for a conference call is equivalent to that of a person-to-person call for each party involved. This service can very often save the cost of travel for face-to-face meetings.

Telex or TWX services are provided by Western Union and the Bell Telephone System. Teletypewriters provide the promptness of a telephone call and the documentation of a letter. These electromagnetic waves can be transmitted 24 hours a day, seven days a week to both domestic and international networks.

Records of times and charges are often required for accounting purposes. Many companies keep complete and accurate records of all toll calls so that the calls can be charged to the clients. Toll charges can be obtained by dialing the operator prior to placing the call and asking the operator to notify you of the toll charges after the call has been completed.

Using the Telephone Effectively

1. Speak directly into the mouthpiece in your normal voice. Your voice is magnified on the telephone, so do not shout.

2. Speak in a clear and alert manner. A flat tone can add distance between you and the listener.

3. Articulate clearly, as the listener cannot infer anything from your body language.

4. Before placing a call, you might want to jot down a few notes so that you can easily recall what you need to say.

5. Maintain a positive attitude toward the listener.

6. Say *please* and *thank you* often.

7. Use the person's name during the conversation; we all like that personal touch.

8. Try to answer by the third ring and be prepared to take a message that includes name, telephone number, message, and time of the call.

9. If a person is on hold, get back to him or her every 30 to 40 seconds so that the person will not feel forgotten.

10. Explain and apologize for long delays.

11. Be discreet about giving out information.

12. Spell any names that may be misunderstood. Clarify letters by saying "A as in apple, B as in boy," and so on.

13. Clarify numbers. For example, 16 and 60 can sound alike. Say, "Sixteen, that is, one six."

14. When placing a call, make certain you have the correct number. Keep up-to-date listings of frequently used numbers.

Telegraph Services

DOMESTIC SERVICES

Regular telegrams can be sent any time of the day or night and are usually deliverable within two hours by telephone with a written confirmation in approximately five hours. They bear a base charge for the first 15 words, with an added charge for each additional word. Your Western Union office can supply you with current rates. Regular telegrams are the most expensive form of domestic telegraph services.

Midnight telegrams can be sent until midnight and are deliverable the following morning. They bear a base charge for the first 100 words with an additional charge for each group of five words. Midnight telegrams are, therefore, recommended for more lengthy messages when there is no urgency involved.

Mailgrams are electronically wired to the post office nearest the recipient. This variation of the midnight telegram also bears a base charge for the first 100 words. The mailgram will be delivered by the mail carrier the next business day and has the advantage of conveying a sense of urgency to the recipient. Mailgrams can be sent via TWX, Telex, Infocom, computer, or voice-originated telephone system.

Collect telegrams can be sent when the recipient will accept the charges.

Telex and TWX services are more fully described in the "Telephone Services" portion of this chapter.

Hotel-motel reservations and confirmations, as well as transportation tickets, are available by telegraph.

Money orders and traveler's checks can be wired to any place in the world. Payment is made by the sender and the recipient need only furnish identification to receive payment.

Candy, flowers and other special occasion items can be sent upon request.

INTERNATIONAL SERVICES

Full-rate cablegrams (FR) provide the fastest service available. They can be sent in any foreign language or code. Rates are based on the distance the message will be transmitted and bear a minimum rate for the first seven words.

Letter telegrams (LT) cannot be sent in code and are delivered the following morning, provided they are placed before midnight. There is a base charge for the first 22 words with an added charge for each additional word. The cost of this service is one-half that of the full-rate cablegram.

Telex services offer a machine-to-machine service. The fee is based on the amount of time used, not the number of words.

TELEGRAM CHARGES

Domestic	International
Each word, regardless of length, counted as one word	Each word determined on the basis of 15 letters to the word
No charge for addresses or one signature	Charge for each word in the address and the signature
No charge for common marks of punctuation	Punctuation marks counted as one word
Symbols counted as mixed group and charged accordingly	Symbols (¢, #, %) must be spelled out because they cannot be transmitted in symbol form

TIPS FOR TYPING THE TELEGRAM

1. Because you are paying per word, wording should be concise and unnecessary words eliminated.

   > Meet you at Kennedy Airport May 2,
   > 2 PM. Arriving TWA, Flight 305.

2. Type an original and two copies. (Blanks are available free of charge from the Western Union office.) The original is for Western Union, a confirmation for the addressee, and a copy for your files.

3. Single space the message using both upper and lower case letters.
4. Indicate the type of service desired and whether the message is to be sent paid, collect, or charge.

PAYMENT OF THE TELEGRAM

A telegram can be:
1. paid with cash at the time the message is sent.
2. charged to a business account.
3. charged to a telephone number.
4. charged to the recipient of the message.

CHAPTER 14

RECORDS MANAGEMENT

Alphabetic Filing, Numerical Filing, Geographic Filing, Subject Filing, Tips for Locating Misplaced Files

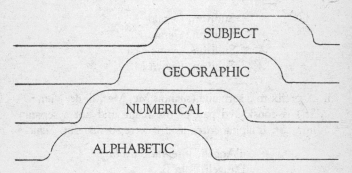

SUBJECT

GEOGRAPHIC

NUMERICAL

ALPHABETIC

If you have ever used the telephone directory, you have applied records management principles. The white pages are arranged in alphabetical order; the pages themselves, in numerical order; the yellow pages, by subject; and each directory, by geographic location.

Uniformity in filing is essential because the filing and instant retrieval of records is the backbone of any organization. The system used must be understood by all who have need for the records.

Alphabetic Filing

NAMES OF INDIVIDUALS

1. To prepare a personal name for filing, place in proper indexing order: surname, first name, middle name or initial.

Sullivan, Thomas Ira

2. Alphabetize names by comparing each unit letter by letter. When names have the same first units,* alphabetize according to the second unit, and so on. A standard rule to remember is: *Nothing comes before something.*

Sullivan, Gerald
Sullivan, Gerald A.
Sullivan, Lynne Mary
Sullivan, Robyn M.

3. A prefix to a surname (such as *Mc, Mac, d, de, Van, O', St.*) is considered part of the name and not a separate unit. *St.* is alphabetized as if it were spelled out, *Saint.*

d'Angeli, Josephine Carla
Dangeli, Rita B.
St. James, James C.
Saint Thomas, William

4. A hyphenated name is considered a single unit and is treated as one name.

Units refers to the sections, or parts, of a name. For example, in *Gerald A.*, *Sullivan* is the first unit; *Gerald*, the second; and

> Harwood, Laura-Beth
> Johns-Allen, Michael

5. Titles, seniority terms, and other designations are dropped from the end of the name for filing purposes. When a married woman's first name is known, use it. When unknown, she is listed as surname, husband's name, *Mrs.*, to distinguish her from her husband.

> Bergstein, Susan
> Bergstein, Warren Mrs.

NAMES OF BUSINESSES AND ORGANIZATIONS

6. Each word of a firm name is treated as a separate unit. When the firm name, however, includes the surname and first name of an individual, transpose the parts of the individual's name.

> Teisch, Morton, Consultant Co.
> Reda Pharmacy, Inc.

7. Articles, conjunctions, and prepositions in English are disregarded for filing purposes. Foreign articles, such as *El*, *La*, *Les*, *Thy*, are included.

> La Pluma Cafe
> (The) Specialty Pastry Shoppe

8. Abbreviations are filed as if written out.

> Geiger Lumber Co.
> Geiger Lumber Company, Inc.

9. Single letters in a name are treated as separate units when they are not known abbreviations.

> ABC Chemical Company
> XYZ Electronics, Inc.

10. Hyphenated firm names are treated as one unit.

> A-B Chemical Company
> Marshall-Dylan Department Store

11. When two names of a business firm can be properly written as one, treat as a single unit.

> Inter National Antiques, Ltd.
> International Jewelry Exchange

12. Numbers in a business firm are filed as if written out and treated as a single unit.

> Eighteen hundred House
> Seven Brothers Associates

13. Compound geographic names are treated as separate units with the exception of *San*, *Los*, and other short foreign names.

> San Francisco Realty Company
> Santa Clara Antiques

14. Banks, hospitals, and religious institutions are listed in the order written.

> Good Samaritan Hospital
> Union State Bank

NAMES OF DOMESTIC AND FOREIGN GOVERNMENTS

15. Branches of the U.S. Government are filed with *U.S. Government* as the first three units. Then comes the department, bureau, division, commission, etc., with the distinctive name of the department considered first.

> U.S. Government, Interior Department
> U.S. Government, Internal Revenue Service

16. State and local governments are filed according to the distinctive name followed by the state, city, etc. Then comes the department, bureau, division, commission, etc. As above, the distinctive part of the department is filed first.

> New Jersey State, Education Department
> New York State, Regents Board

17. To index foreign governments, consider the dominion, kingdom, etc. first followed by the name of the country. Then proceed as you would with domestic governments.

> Denmark, Kingdom, State Department
> Germany, Federal Republic, State Department

Numerical Filing

Numerical filing, the arrangement of records according to numbers, has the following advantages:

1. Names can be identical; numbers cannot.
2. Files can be expanded more easily because you can add

storage units as necessary. In the other filing systems, it may be necessary to rearrange complete files as drawers become too crowded.

3. Confidentiality is increased because numbers are impersonal in nature.
4. Many systems make use of numbers already in use, such as social security numbers, telephone numbers, and account numbers.

Numerical filing is managed in three different ways:

CONSECUTIVE NUMBER FILING

This system is used primarily when the identifying numbers contain no more than four digits. The numbers are read from left to right with higher numbers filed behind lower ones.

1234
1235
1236

MIDDLE DIGIT FILING

This system is primarily used when numbers are grouped in three units. The group in the middle is considered the first unit (1); the group on the left, the second unit (2); and the group on the right, the third unit (3). Note: Although you are sequencing according to the middle digits, do not change the order of the numbers.

2	1	3
06	15	791
07	15	158
56	26	730
01	28	033

TERMINAL DIGIT FILING

This system is primarily used when numbers are grouped in units. The group to the right is the first unit and the units are thereafter read from right to left.

3	2	1
01	28	033
07	15	158
56	26	730
06	15	791

Geographic Filing

Geographic filing, the arrangement of records according to location, is used when this is the most efficient means for a company. Sales organization and manufacturers employ this system to indicate domestic and/or international territories and utility companies use it to indicate customer locations.

An international system categorizes according to the name of the country; a domestic system categorizes according to the name of the state. Following the state, the city is considered, and then the name of the company.

New York, Albany, James & Sons, Inc.
New York, Albany, Zone Planning Enterprises
New York, Buffalo, A & S Stationery Supplies
Virginia, Richmond, Local Contractors, Inc.
Virginia, Suffolk, AAA Auto Supplies
   Company

Subject Filing

Subject filing, the arrangement of records according to topics, is used when it is expedient for a company to file according to topics such as items, objects, business activities, and functions.

The sequencing of these files is like that found in the yellow pages of your telephone directory.

Physicians	Leon Andersen, M.D.
	Michael Cavanagh, M.D.
	Isadore Sternlieb, M.D.
Schools	Elmwood Elementary School
	Spring Valley Junior High School
	Spring Valley Senior High School

Tips for Locating Misplaced Files

1. Look on your employer's desk and in his/her briefcase, and ask others who use the file.
2. Look in the file folder in front of and in back of the missing one. It might have been placed inadvertently in one of these folders.
3. If your office uses an alphabetic filing system, look under various spellings of the name. In a numerical filing system, look under various numerical arrangements. In a geographic filing system, look under the same or similar names in other cities and/or states. For a lost file in a subject filing system, look under related headings. For *janitorial services*, for instance, look under *maintenance*.

CHAPTER 15

TIMELY TIPS

Taking Dictation, Proofreading, Erasures and Corrections

Taking Dictation

1. Before you leave your desk to take dictation for an extended period of time, put away all confidential material. Also, make certain that no transcript of a confidential nature is left exposed in your typewriter.
2. If you regularly take dictation from more than one person, retain a separate notebook and portfolio for each so that the work will not become confused.
3. Keep your supplies in one place so that you do not have to go searching.
4. Supplies should include:
   a. A spiral-bound notebook. Make certain that you have enough pages left in your notebook for the amount of dictation you anticipate. If in doubt, have an extra book ready.
   b. Two pens that do not leave ink blobs. Some shorthand writers prefer thin-tipped felt markers because they require less pressure. An extra writing instrument should always be available in case the first one runs dry.

    c. A colored pencil. Red is preferable so that it can be used for emphasis whenever you feel it necessary.

    d. Two or three paper clips. They can be placed on any page or pages to indicate rush items or a task that must be taken care of following the dictation. *Write everything down*; do not rely on your memory.

    e. A rubber band. Place it around all used pages so that you can open to the next clean page without wasting time.

    f. A pocket-sized calendar. This can be taped to the inside cover for easy reference while taking dictation.

5. Always indicate on the notebook cover the dates of your first and last entries, and retain used books for a period of one or two months. It may be necessary to refer to past dictation or a past notation.

6. If you have an employer who makes constant changes in dictation, it may be wise to use the left side of the notebook for dictation and the right side for changes of notations.

7. Listen carefully for pauses in the dictator's voice; a pause will often indicate that a mark of punctuation is necessary.

8. If the dictator has dictated something incorrectly and you discover it during the transcription period, be sure to ask about it. If the dictator is not available, make the change. Your employer will make mistakes (we all do), but he/she is paying you to turn out mailable and correct transcripts.

9. Utilize interruptions (telephone calls, visitors) to review your notes. You can insert punctuation and make a note of any word(s) you feel you may have difficulty transcribing. After the interruption, you can ask the dictator about any source of confusion. Also, be prepared to read back the last sentence or two so that the dictator can recapture his/her thought process.

10. When the dictator spells out a proper name or an unusually

spelled word, write it in longhand so that you will spell it correctly when you transcribe.

11. Place a diagonal line through any notes that you have transcribed or any assignment you have completed.

12. Always prioritize your work. Certain assignments are more important than others and should be transcribed first.

Proofreading

Many a lawsuit has been instituted due to a discrepancy that should have been detected by a skillfull proofreader. It is essential that you carefully proofread everything you type, keeping in mind the following:

1. Do not remove your transcript from the typewriter until you have checked it carefully. Corrections are much easier to make if you do not have to align.

2. Scan the overall transcript to make certain that the format and styling are correct.

3. Accurately pinpoint any typographical, punctuation, or grammatical errors.

4. Double check the spelling of all names and make certain that initials are correct.

5. Check the accuracy of all numbers, addresses, amounts of money, dates, and any other information that is easily miscopied.

6. Check the continuity of all numbered pages and paragraphs.

7. If you are proofreading technical or statistical information, the buddy system is recommended. If possible, give the copy you typed to another person and read from the original. Carefully pronounce word endings (s, ing, ed) and spell any unusually spelled names. Repeat numbers indi-

vidually. For instance, 6,789 should be read "six, seven, eight, nine."

8. When proofreading technical or statistical information alone, place the original and transcript side by side and, with a ruler or envelope, follow line by line.

9. Reread the transcript a second time. It is sometimes easier to detect errors when you read the carbon copy as a second review.

Erasures and Corrections

Every efficient secretary must perfect the skill of making corrections. Most offices use erasable bond paper, so the task has been greatly simplified.

Several correction methods are available:

Erasers Your eraser should always be clean in order to prevent smudge marks. You can clean an eraser by rubbing the soiled spot on a clean sheet of paper. Make corrections on the original and all carbon copies. To prevent the carbon copies from smudging, use either a steel eraser guard or a sheet of paper between the carbon paper and the copy paper.

In order to prevent the removal of surrounding letters, use an erasing shield (as pictured on page 243). They can be purchased at most stationery or typing-supply stores.

Chalk-coated paper Correction paper is available in white as well as a wide variety of colors to match any stationery and copy paper. Its use is simple. Backspace to the typographical error, insert the correction paper, hit the incorrect key, remove the correction paper, then backspace and strike the correct key.

Correction fluid Correction fluid is available in white and a variety of pastel colors. It can be purchased from the manufacturer to match any office stationery. Its application is also simple. Brush it over the error lightly and wait a moment for it to dry. After the liquid has dried, you can type the correct information. This method should not be overused.

Correction strip Many documents are typed strictly for reproduction purposes. In such cases, when you have detected an error that encompasses a sentence, a paragraph, or more, you can type the correct information on a separate sheet of paper and tape it over the incorrect information. When the instrument is photocopied, no one will be the wiser.

Correction ribbon cartridge This technique is easily accomplished by removing the typewriter ribbon cartridge and inserting a special cartridge containing correction tape. Correct as you would when using the chalk-coated paper, then reinsert the typewriter ribbon cartridge.

Self-correcting typewriter On the self-correcting typewriter it is easy to make corrections when special adhesive ribbon is used. The ribbon allows you to make a correction by depressing the special backspace key and striking over the incorrect character(s). Once the incorrect information has been removed, continue your typing. This method will only work if you have not proceeded to the next line. If you have done so, special coding will be necessary to bring you back to the correction point.

Squeezing and spreading If your typewriter has a half-space key, squeezing and spreading is an easy task. If not, this technique can be accomplished by moving the carriage or element one-half space to the left and squeezing or spreading the necessary letter or letters.

collection   e x p a n d

When these corrections appear in the body of a text, they are not obvious.

All corrections must be neatly accomplished on all copies. If you find that an erasure is easily detectable, it has not been properly corrected and the page should be retyped. To retype a page, copy from the original and not the corrected copy. This avoids the possibility of making the same error again.

There may be instances when you have stapled several pieces of paper at the top and notice a mistake on the second or third page. The error can be easily corrected without removing the staples.

   a. Insert a large envelope into your typewriter and roll it forward until an inch of the envelope is visible.

   b. From the front, insert the page that contains the error. Place the bottom edge of the page between the envelope and the platen (roller).

   c. Turn the platen in reverse motion so that the page is drawn into the machine.

   d. Align the page and begin typing.

CORRECTION METHODS — ADVANTAGES AND DISADVANTAGES

	ERASER	CORRECTION FLUIDS		CORRECTION PAPER	CORRECTION RIBBON	CORRECTING TYPEWRITER
		CHEMICAL	WATER-BASE			
TIME REQUIRED	Done correctly, the most time consuming method.	Fast-dry formula dries in 10-12 secs.	Takes about 45 secs. to dry.	Extra backspace time is needed.	Extra backspace time is needed.	Fast.
PERMANENCY	Permanent.	Permanent.	Permanent.	Temporary; chalky substance may flake off in mail or file.	Temporary; chalky substance may flake off in mail or file.	Permanent.
EFFECT ON PAPER	Makes indention on paper surface; can make paper fuzzy.	Bonds itself to paper making like-new surface for typing.	Bonds itself to paper making like-new surface for typing.	Chalk-like substance adheres to paper.	Chalk-like substance adheres to paper.	Lifts carbon ink off paper, or covers carbon ink with chalk-like substance.
TECHNIQUE INVOLVED	Practice needed to acquire technique.	Practice needed to acquire technique.	Practice needed to acquire technique.	Little technique needed.	No technique needed.	Knowledge of correcting typewriter required.
MATERIALS REQUIRED	Eraser, index cards, type cleaner, metal letter protector.	Bottle of correction fluid, thinner.	Bottle of correction fluid.	Appropriate type of correction paper for paper being corrected.	Correction ribbon.	Self-correcting typewriter, special ribbons.
CORRECTIONS ON COLORED PAPER	Many times erases pigment; spots.	Comes in white and colors.	Comes in white and colors.	Comes in white and limited colors.	Comes in white only.	Corrects on all colors.
OTHER POSSIBLE CORRECTIONS	Corrects typewritten or pen errors; corrects before or after removed from typewriter.	Corrects typewritten or pen errors; corrects before or after removed from typewriter.	Corrects typewritten or pen errors; corrects before or after removed from typewriter.	Corrects only typewritten errors; once removed from typewriter, very difficult to reinsert.	Corrects only typewritten errors; once removed from typewriter, very difficult to reinsert.	Corrects only typewritten errors; once removed from typewriter, very difficult to reinsert.
CARBON COPIES/ PHOTOCOPIES	Corrects carbon copies; smears chemical surface on some photocopies.	Corrects carbon copies; can smear some photocopies.	Corrects carbon copies; will not smear photocopies.	Corrects carbon copies; will not correct photocopies.	Will not correct carbon copies or photocopies.	Will not correct carbon copies or photocopies.

Part III.
Professional
Potpourri

CHAPTER 16

FORMS OF ADDRESS

Government Officials, Military Personnel, Religious Officials, Education Officials

Government Officials

Person	Salutation	Closing
The President	Dear Mr./Mrs./Ms. President: Mr./Mrs./Ms. President:	Respectfully yours,
The Vice-President	Dear Mr./Mrs./Ms. Vice-President: Mr./Mrs./Ms. Vice-President:	Respectfully yours,
Chief Justice	Dear Mr./Madam Chief Justice: Sir/Madam:	Very truly yours, Sincerely yours,
Cabinet Officers	Dear Mr./Madam Secretary: The Honorable...:	Very truly yours, Sincerely yours,
Senators	Dear Senator...: The Honorable...:	Very truly yours, Sincerely yours,
Representative	The Honorable...: Sir/Madam:	Very truly yours, Sincerely yours,

Governor	Dear Governor....: Sir/Madam:	Respectfully yours, Very sincerely yours,
State Senator	Dear Senator....: Sir/Madam:	Very truly yours, Sincerely yours,
State Representative	Dear Mr./Mrs./Ms. ....: Sir/Madam:	Very truly yours, Sincerely yours,
Mayor	Dear Mayor....: Dear Sir/Madam:	Very truly yours, Sincerely yours,
Ambassador	Dear Mr./Madam Ambassador: Sir/Madam:	Very truly yours, Sincerely yours,
Minister	Dear Mr./Madam Minister: Sir/Madam:	Very truly yours, Sincerely yours,

Military Personnel

Person	Salutation	Closing
General, USA*	Dear General . . . : Sir/Madam:	Very truly yours, Sincerely yours,
Lieutenant General	Dear General . . . : Sir/Madam:	Very truly yours, Sincerely yours,
Colonel	Dear Colonel:	Very truly yours, Sincerely yours,
Major	Dear Major . . . :	Very truly yours, Sincerely yours,
Captain	Dear Captain . . . :	Very truly yours, Sincerely yours,

*United States Army.

Admiral, USN	Dear Admiral....:	Very truly yours, Sincerely yours,
Chaplain	Dear Chaplain....:	Very truly yours, Sincerely yours,

Religious Officials

Cardinal	Dear Cardinal...: Your Eminence:	Respectfully, Sincerely yours,
Archbishop	Dear Archbishop....: Your Excellency:	Respectfully, Sincerely yours,
Bishop	Dear Bishop....: Your Excellency:	Respectfully, Sincerely yours,
Monsignor	Dear Monsignor....: Right Reverend Monsignor	Respectfully yours, Sincerely yours,

Person	Salutation	Closing
Priest	Reverend Father: Dear Father . . . :	Respectfully, Sincerely yours,
Mother Superior	Dear Reverend Mother: Dear Mother . . . :	Respectfully, Sincerely yours,
Sister	Dear Sister . . . : Dear Sister:	Respectfully, Sincerely yours,
Reverend	Reverend Sir:	Respectfully yours, Sincerely yours,
Rabbi	Dear Rabbi . . . : Sir:	Respectfully yours, Sincerely yours,

Education Officials

Person	Salutation	Closing
President	Dear Dr. . . . : Sir/Madam:	Very truly yours, Sincerely yours,

Dean	Dear Dean....: Dear Sir/Madam:	Very truly yours, Sincerely yours,
Professor	Dear Professor....: Dear Sir/Madam:	Very truly yours, Sincerely yours,
Instructor	Dear Mr.....: Dear Sir/Madam:	Very truly yours, Sincerely yours,

CHAPTER 17

WORD PROCESSING TERMINOLOGY

Word processing (WP) is a highly sophisticated system that integrates people, procedures, and equipment. The U.S. Bureau of Statistics has predicted that the projected increase in information processing will necessitate a 30 percent expansion in secretarial personnel over the next several years. An understanding of WP terminology will put you one step closer to a system that is revolutionizing the modern office.

administrative secretary	one who performs all clerical nontyping tasks
alphanumeric	a combination of alphabetic and numerical characters
automatic equipment	equipment that performs many tasks such as centering, carriage return, line spacing, and centering either automatically or by key-stroke command
basic document cycle	creation, storage, use, transfer, and disposal of a record
batch	a collection of similar work that can be produced in a single operation
bit	the smallest unit of information

byte	a sequence of bits, usually shorter than a word
career path	opportunities available for advancement
cassette	a plastic or metal cartridge used in recording information
character	a letter, number, or symbol
cluster	a work group or unit of employees and/or equipment
COM	computer output microfilm
command	instruction of the WP machine to perform a certain function
communicating typewriter	equipment that can send and receive information with another communicating typewriter via telephone hookups
correspondence secretary	one who performs all typing tasks
CPS	characters per second
CPU	central processing unit
crash	disk down (inoperable)
CRT	cathode ray tube, a TV-like screen for the display of characters
cursor	a movable indicator on a CRT which indicates the place for editing a document
daisy print wheel	a printing element, resembling a flattened daisy, that has a character at the end of each petal
data base	files of information used by an organization
delete	instruction to remove a character, a word, a line, or more from a document

discrete media	belts, disks, cartridges, and cassettes that are removable for storage
disk (or diskette or disc)	WP machine equipment used for recording, transcribing, and storing data
down	equipment inoperable
edit	to revise a text
element	a removable, replaceable printer
endless loop	a sealed, continuous loop inside a tank that allows for simultaneous dictating and transcribing
facsimile (FAX)	the transmission and reception of textual copy through telephone lines
flowchart	a system of diagrams and symbols sequencing the progression of work from origin to completion
floppy disk	a pliable type of disk
font	an assortment of characters in one type size and style
hard copy	typed or printed texts
hardware	word processing equipment
hot zone	the area in which editing equipment will determine where the right-hand margin should be
ink jet printer	a printing device that electronically squirts ink onto paper in character form
input	information entered into a system for processing
I/O	input/output device
IWP	International Word Processing Association, an association that deals with systems and methods of word processing

job description	a written description of each worker's duties and responsibilities
keyboarding	typewriting
logging	a method of recording incoming and outgoing work in order to monitor its flow
menu	selection of tasks
OCR	optical character recognition
off-line	equipment not connected to or dependent on peripheral equipment
on-line	equipment connected to and dependent on peripheral equipment
output	the final results produced
PBX	private branch exchange (telephone system)
peripheral equipment	equipment that works with the central unit, such as keyboards and printers
pitch	the number of characters per horizontal inch (10 on a pica and 12 on an elite)
principal	the originator of a document who requires secretarial support
procedures manual	a manual that gives the step-by-step process for completing a certain task
reprographics	reproduction of a document
search	a command given to locate automatically previously recorded information
shared logic	a system that allows two or more units to utilize the memory of a single CPU
software	programs and routines needed to use hardware
stand-alone unit	a self-contained, independent unit

station	the work location for a WP operator
store	to place in memory information not subject to change
terminal	a device that can send and receive information
text-editing equipment	a WP typewriter capable of revising texts
time-sharing	the simultaneous use of the CPU
traditional secretary	an all-purpose secretary responsible for typing and nontyping tasks
turnaround time	the time that elapses from the beginning to the completion of a task
variable	a segment of a document subject to change
VOR	voice operated relay, a device that activates a recorder when it senses that a voice is coming over the line
WP system	the combination of people, procedures, and equipment that constitutes a total support system

CHAPTER 18

CHARTS AND TABLES

Anniversary List, Birthday List, Decimal Equivalents of Fractions, Foreign Currency, Foreign Words and Phrases, Legal Holidays and Celebrations, Mathematical Computations, Proofreader's Marks, Signs and Symbols, Signs of the Zodiac, State Capitals and Flowers, Weights and Measures

Anniversary List

Year	Traditional	Modern
first	paper	clocks
second	cotton	china
third	leather	crystal
fourth	fruit, flowers	appliances
fifth	wood	silverware
sixth	candy, iron	wood
seventh	copper, wool	desk sets
eighth	bronze, pottery	linens, lace
ninth	pottery, willow	leather
tenth	tin, aluminum	diamond jewelry
eleventh	steel	fashion jewelry

twelfth	silk, linen	pearls
thirteenth	lace	textiles, fur
fourteenth	ivory	gold jewelry
fifteenth	crystal	watches
twentieth	china	platinum
twenty-fifth	silver	silver
thirtieth	pearls	diamonds
thirty-fifth	coral	jade
fortieth	rubies	rubies
fiftieth	gold	gold
fifty-fifth	emeralds	emeralds
sixtieth	diamonds	diamonds
seventy-fifth	diamonds	diamonds

Birthday List

Month	Birthstone	Flower
January	garnet	carnation
February	amethyst	violet
March	aquamarine	jonquil
April	diamond	sweat pea
May	emerald	lily of the valley
June	pearl and alexandrite	rose
July	ruby	larkspur
August	peridot and sardonyx	gladiolus
September	sapphire	aster
October	opal and tourmaline	calendula
November	topaz	chrysanthemum
December	turquoise and zircon	narcissus

Decimal Equivalents of Fractions

½ = .50		⅖ = .33333	
⅓ = .33333		⅗ = .50	
⅔ = .66667		⅘ = .66667	
¼ = .25		⅚ = .83333	
²⁄₄ = .50		⅛ = .125	
¾ = .75		²⁄₈ = .25	
⅕ = .20		⅜ = .375	
⅖ = .40		⁴⁄₈ = .50	
⅗ = .60		⅝ = .625	
⅘ = .80		⁶⁄₈ = .75	
⅙ = .16667		⅞ = .875	

Foreign Currency

Country	Monetary Unit
Argentina	peso
Australia	Australian pound
Austria	schilling
Belgium	franc
Bolivia	boliviano
Brazil	cruziero
British Honduras	dollar
Bulgaria	lev (leva)
Burma	kvat
Canada	Canadian dollar
Ceylon	rupee
Chile	peso
China	People's yuan

Columbia	peso
Costa Rica	colón
Cuba	peso
Czechoslovakia	koruna
Denmark	krone (kroner)
Dominican Republic	peso
Ecuador	sucre
Egypt	Egyptian pound
El Salvador	colón
Ethiopia	Ethiopian dollar
Finland	markka
France	franc
Germany (East)	mark
Germany (West)	Deutsche mark
Great Britain (England)	pound sterling
Greece	drachma
Guatemala	quetzal
Haiti	gourde
Honduras	lempira
Hungary	forint
Iceland	króna (krónur)
India	rupee
Indonesia	rupiah
Iran	rial
Iraq	Iraqi dinar
Ireland	pound sterling
Israel	Israeli pound
Italy	lira
Japan	yen
Jordan	Jordan dinar
Korea	hwan
Lebanon	Lebanese pound
Liberia	Liberian dollar
Libya	Libyan pound
Luxembourg	franc

Malaya	Malayan dollar
Mexico	peso
Netherlands (Holland)	guilder
New Zealand	New Zealand pound
Nicaragua	córdoba
Norway	krone (kroner)
Pakistan	Pakistan rupee
Panama	balboa
Paraguay	guaraní
Peru	sol
Philippines	peso
Poland	zloty
Portugal	escudo
Romania	leu
Russia (U.S.S.R.)	ruble
Saudi Arabia	riyal
South Africa	rand
Spain	peseta
Sweden	krona
Switzerland	Swiss franc
Syria	Syrian pound
Taiwan	New Taiwan dollar
Thailand	baht
Turkey	lira
Uruguay	peso
Venezuela	bolivar
Yugoslavia	dinar

Foreign Words and Phrases

Word or Phrase	Meaning
ad hoc	committee for a special purpose
à la mode	in the style

alma mater	a school one has attended
attaché	member of a diplomatic staff
avant-garde	ahead of its time
blasé	apathetic to pleasure
bona fide	genuine
bon appétit	hearty appetite
bonjour	good day, hello
bon vivant	one who enjoys the good life
carte blanche	full authority
caveat emptor	let the buyer beware
coup d'état	take over of a government
circa	approximately
crème de la crème	the best
cum laude	with distinction
de facto	in reality
de jure	by right, by law
dossier	file of detailed information
emeritus	honorary rank after retirement
en masse	all together
entrée	main course of meal, method of access
entrepreneur	one who manages and assumes the risk in a business
ergo	therefore
esprit de corps	group enthusiasm, morale
ex officio	by position of office
ex parte	one side of a proceeding
ex post facto	after the fact
faux pas	social blunder
habeus corpus	a writ ordering a party to be brought before the court
hoi polloi	the common people, masses
hors d'oeuvre	appetizer
idem	the same
in loco parentis	temporary parental authority
in personam	action against a person

ipso facto	by the fact itself
laissez-faire	let one do as one chooses
maitre d'	headwaiter
modus operandi	method of operation
nunc pro tunc	now for then
per annum	by the year
per capita	by the individual
per diem	by the day
per se	by itself
post mortem	after death
potpourri	a miscellaneous collection
prima facie	first view
pro rata	according to the rate
quid pro quo	something in return
raison d'être	reason for existing
rendezvous	appointed meeting place
resumé	an account of one's qualifications
status quo	an existing state of affairs
tort	a wrongdoing that is not a breach of contract
verbatim	word for word
vice versa	conversely
vis-à-vis	face to face

Many of the diacritical marks used in foreign words must be inserted by hand because they do not appear on the keyboard of a standard typewriter. Such special keys are available, however, and are useful to have if you need them frequently.

- ´ acute accent (French, Spanish)
- ` grave accent (French, Italian)
- ^ circumflex (French)
- ¨ dieresis (French, English) or umlaut (German)
- ~ tilde (Spanish)
- ¸ cedilla (French)

Legal Holidays and Celebrations

Holiday	Date
New Year's Day	January 1
Groundhog Day	February 2
Lincoln's Birthday	February 12
Valentine's Day	February 14
Washington's Birthday	February 22*
St. Patrick's Day	March 17
Good Friday	Friday before Easter Sunday
Mother's Day	second Sunday in May
Memorial Day	last Monday in May
Father's Day	third Sunday in June
Flag Day	June 14
Independence Day	July 4
Labor Day	first Monday in September
Columbus Day	October 12*
Halloween	October 31
Election Day	first Tuesday following first Monday in November
Veteran's Day	November 11
Thanksgiving	fourth Thursday in November
Christmas	December 25

The holidays not listed are those that fluctuate.

> Thirty days has September, April, June, and
> November,
> All the rest have thirty-one,
> Except February, which alone has twenty-eight,
> Until leap year gives it twenty-nine.

---

*Traditional date; the date on which the holiday is observed varies.

Mathematical Computations

Area
circle = square of diameter × .785398
ellipse = long diameter × short diameter × .7854
parallelogram = base × height
rectangle = side × side
right triangle = ½ base × altitude
sector of circle = radius squared × 3.14159265
triangle = ½ base × altitude

Circle
circumference = diameter × 3.14159265
diameter = circumference × .3183

Interest
$$\frac{\text{Principal} \times \text{Rate} \times \text{Time}}{360 \text{ or } 365 \text{ days}} = \text{Interest}$$

Merchandise Markup
based on cost
selling price = cost + (markup % × cost)
based on selling price
selling price = cost ÷ cost % of selling price
markup
markup = selling price − cost

Payroll
gross pay − deductions = net pay (take home)

Proofreader's Marks

    transpose

We would ^like your input	insert word(s)
In our judgement, we would	delete
The President ~~has asked~~ *stet*	retain deleted material
stomach#ache	leave space between words
ear‿ache	close space between words
Their ^lc Accounting ^lc Department	lower case
Star wars or Star Wars	capitalize, upper case
We would like to ^ss have your opinion regarding the sale	single space
We would like to ^DS have ^DS your opinion regarding the sale	double space
a very ~~well-known~~ man	remove underscore
Fed. (sp)	spell out fully
⌐5⌐ Now is the time	indent (five spaces)

we have been.⁋ This
would   new paragraph

noⁿ This would have
been   no new paragraph

→TOTALS←   center on page

Who and Whom   boldface type

᭫ apostrophe   (;) semicolon

[ ] brackets   ⌐⌐ move up

(:) colon   ⌐⌐ move down

↑ comma   ⊏ move to the left

✗ ✗ ✗ ellipsis   ⊐ move to the right

(!) exclamation   ‖ align type
    point

⊝ hyphen   *wf* wrong font

( ) parentheses   ⌒ run in material

⊙ period   (?) verify information

(?) question   *ital* italicize
    mark

" " quotation
    marks

Signs and Symbols

@	at, each	4 dozen @ 15 cents
#	number sign	#10249
%	percent	100%
¢	cents	75¢
&	ampersand	Smith & Smith
*	asterisk	in the book.*
'	feet or minutes	20'
"	inches, seconds, ditto	56"
®	registered trademark	®
+	plus	5 + 5
=	equals	5 + 5 = 10
±	plus or minus	±15
∓	minus or plus	∓15
×	multiply	1 × 2
÷	divide	15 ÷ 3
>	greater than	25 > 24
<	less than	24 < 25

Signs of the Zodiac

March 21–April 19	Aries	the Ram
April 20–May 20	Taurus	the Bull
May 21–June 20	Gemini	the Twins
June 21–July 22	Cancer	the Crab
July 23–August 22	Leo	the Lion
August 23–September 22	Virgo	the Virgin
September 23–October 22	Libra	the Balance
October 23–November 21	Scorpio	the Scorpion
November 22–December 21	Sagittarius	the Archer

December 22–January 19	Capricorn	the Goat
January 20–February 18	Aquarius	the Water-bearer
February 19–March 20	Pisces	the Fish

State Capitals and Flowers

State	Capital	Flower
Alabama	Montgomery	camellia
Alaska	Juneau	forget-me-not
Arizona	Phoenix	saguaro (cactus)
Arkansas	Little Rock	apple blossom
California	Sacramento	golden poppy
Colorado	Denver	blue columbine
Connecticut	Hartford	mountain laurel
Delaware	Dover	peach blossom
District of Columbia	Washington	American beauty rose
Florida	Tallahassee	orange blossom
Georgia	Atlanta	Cherokee rose
Hawaii	Honolulu	red hibiscus
Idaho	Boise	syringa
Illinois	Springfield	wood violet
Indiana	Indianapolis	peony
Iowa	Des Moines	wild rose
Kansas	Topeka	sunflower
Kentucky	Frankfort	goldenrod
Louisiana	Baton Rouge	magnolia
Maine	Augusta	pine cone
Maryland	Annapolis	black-eyed Susan
Massachusetts	Boston	mayflower
Michigan	Lansing	apple blossom
Minnesota	St. Paul	moccasin flower

Mississippi	Jackson	magnolia
Missouri	Jefferson City	hawthorn
Montana	Helena	bitterroot
Nebraska	Lincoln	goldenrod
Nevada	Carson City	sagebrush
New Hampshire	Concord	purple lilac
New Jersey	Trenton	purple violet
New Mexico	Santa Fe	yucca
New York	Albany	rose (any color)
North Carolina	Raleigh	dogwood
North Dakota	Bismarck	wild prairie rose
Ohio	Columbus	scarlet carnation
Oklahoma	Oklahoma City	mistletoe
Oregon	Salem	Oregon grape
Pennsylvania	Harrisburg	mountain laurel
Rhode Island	Providence	violet
South Carolina	Columbia	Carolina jessamine
South Dakota	Pierre	pasque flower
Tennessee	Nashville	iris
Texas	Austin	bluebonnet
Utah	Salt Lake City	sego lily
Vermont	Montpelier	red clover
Virginia	Richmond	American dogwood
Washington	Olympia	pink rhododendron
West Virginia	Charleston	big rhododendron
Wisconsin	Madison	wood violet
Wyoming	Cheyenne	Indian paintbrush

Weights and Measures

Unit	Abbre- viation	Same System Equivalent	Metric Equivalent
ton		2000 pounds	0.907 metric tons
pound	lb/#	16 ounces	0.453 kilograms
ounce	oz/oz av	16 drams	28.349 grams
dram	dr/dr av	0.0625 ounces	1.771 grams
grain	gr	0.036 drams	0.0648 grams

Capacity

gallon	gal	4 quarts	3.785 liters
quart	qt	2 pints	0.946 liters
pint	pt	4 gills	0.473 liters
gill	gi	4 fluid ounces	118.291 milliliters
fluid ounce	fl oz	8 fluid drams	29.573 milliliters
fluid dram	fl dr	60 minims	3.696 milliliters
minim	min	1/60 fl dr	0.061610 millileters

Dry Measure

bushel	bu	4 pecks	35.238 liters
peck	pk	8 quarts	8.809 liters
quart	qt	2 pints	1.101 liters
pint	pt	.5 quart	0.550 liters

Length

mile	mi	5280 feet	1.609 kilometers
rod	rd	16.5 feet	5.029 meters
yard	yd	3 feet	0.9144 meters
foot	ft/'	12 inches	30.480 centimeters
inch	in/"	0.083 feet	2.540 centimeters

Area

square mile	sq mi	640 acres	2.590 sq kilometers
acre		4840 sq yd	4047 sq meters
square rod	sq rd	0.006 acres	25.293 sq meters
square yard	sq yd	9 sq ft	0.836 sq meters
square foot	sq ft	0.111 sq yd	0.093 sq meters
square inch	sq in	0.007 sq ft	6.451 sq centimeters

Volume

cubic yard	cu yd	27 cu ft	0.765 cu meters
cubic foot	cu ft	1728 cu in	0.028 cu meters
cubic inch	cu in	0.00058 cu ft	16.387 cu centimeters

CONVERSION TABLE

1 inch = 25 millimeters	1 millimeter = 0.04 inch
1 inch = 2.5 centimeters	1 centimeter = 0.4 inch
1 foot = 0.3 meter	1 meter = 3.3 feet
1 yard = 0.9 meter	1 meter = 1.1 yards

TEMPERATURE TABLE

32° Fahrenheit (F)	=	0° Celsius (C)	(freezing point of water)
212° Fahrenheit	=	100° Celsius	(boiling point of water)
98.6° Fahrenheit	=	37° Celsius	(normal body temperature)

INDEX

277